JOURNAL FOR THE STUDY OF THE NEW TESTAMENT SUPPLEMENT SERIES
209

Executive Editor
Stanley E. Porter

Sheffield Academic Press
A Continuum imprint

Going Outside the Camp

The Sociological Function of
the Levitical Critique in
the Epistle to the Hebrews

Richard W. Johnson

Journal for the Study of the New Testament
Supplement Series 209

British Library Cataloguing-in-Publication Data

A catalogue record for this book is available from the British Library

Typeset by Sheffield Academic Press
Printed on acid-free paper in Great Britain by MPG Books Ltd,
Bodmin, Cornwall

ISBN 1-84127-186-1

To the memory of Ronald Johnson and to Janice Evans Johnson,
my parents, who instilled in me a love of learning;

To my wife, Susan Dieter Johnson,
whose support has made my scholarly adventure possible;

To my daughter, Sarah Rachel Johnson,
who fills my days with joy.

CONTENTS

LIST OF TABLES

LIST OF FIGURES

ACKNOWLEDGMENTS

The publication of this work is the result of the contributions of an uncountably finite number of people. My parents, my wife, and my daughter stand in the background of all that I do. Charles A. Ray Jr and William F. Warren Jr, my mentors, were extraordinarily generous with their time, wisdom, and encouragement. George H. Guthrie was gracious in assisting me to sharpen my thoughts as we discussed (sometimes passionately) the purpose of Hebrews. My colleagues at Charleston Southern University welcomed me into my professional home. Without the diligent labors of the many professionals at Sheffield Academic Press, the manuscript would have gone unpublished. To these, and to many more whom I have left unnamed, a heart-felt 'Thank you'.

ABBREVIATIONS

AB	Anchor Bible
ABD	David Noel Freedman (ed.), *The Anchor Bible Dictionary* (6 vols.; New York: Doubleday, 1992)
AGJU	Arbeiten zur Geschichte des antiken Judentums und des Urchristentums
ATR	*Anglican Theological Review*
AUSS	*Andrews University Seminary Studies*
BA	*Biblical Archaeologist*
Bib	*Biblica*
CBQ	*Catholic Biblical Quarterly*
CRINT	Compendia rerum iudaicarum ad Novum Testamentum
CurTM	*Currents in Theology and Mission*
ETL	*Ephemerides theologicae lovanienses*
EvQ	*Evangelical Quarterly*
ExpTim	*Expository Times*
HR	*History of Religions*
HTR	*Harvard Theological Review*
ICC	International Critical Commentary
Int	*Interpretation*
JBL	*Journal of Biblical Literature*
JJS	*Journal of Jewish Studies*
JSJ	*Journal for the Study of Judaism in the Persian, Hellenistic and Roman Period*
JSNT	*Journal for the Study of the New Testament*
JSNTSup	*Journal for the Study of the New Testament*, Supplement Series
JSOT	*Journal for the Study of the Old Testament*
JSS	*Journal of Semitic Studies*
LCL	Loeb Classical Library
NICNT	New International Commentary on the New Testament
NICOT	New International Commentary on the Old Testament
NIGTC	The New International Greek Testament Commentary
NovTSup	*Novum Testamentum*, Supplements
NTS	*New Testament Studies*
OTP	James Charlesworth (ed.), *Old Testament Pseudepigrapha*
RB	*Revue biblique*

RelSRev	*Religious Studies Review*
ResQ	*Restoration Quarterly*
RevExp	*Review and Expositor*
RevistB	*Revista bíblica*
RevQ	*Revue de Qumrân*
RHPR	*Revue d'histoire et de philosophie religieuses*
RSR	*Recherche de science religieuse*
RTR	*Reformed Theological Review*
ScEs	*Science et Esprit*
SBLDS	SBL Dissertation Series
SBLSP	SBL Seminar Papers
SJLA	Studies in Judaism in Late Antiquity
SJT	*Scottish Journal of Theology*
SNTSMS	Society for New Testament Studies Monograph Series
SR	*Studies in Religion/Sciences religieuses*
TDNT	Gerhard Kittel and Gerhard Friedrich (eds.), *Theological Dictionary of the New Testament* (trans. Geoffrey W. Bromiley; 9 vols; Grand Rapids: Eerdmans, 1964–1974)
TynBul	*Tyndale Bulletin*
TZ	*Theologische Zeitschrift*
VC	*Vigiliae christianae*
WBC	Word Biblical Commentary

Chapter 1

INTRODUCTION

Polybius, writing in the second century BCE, grasped the sociological function of religion. 'The quality in which the Roman commonwealth is most distinctly superior is in my opinion the nature of their religious convictions. I believe that it is the very thing…which maintains the cohesion of the Roman State… For this reason I think, not that the ancients acted rashly and at haphazard in introducing among the people notions concerning the gods and beliefs in the terrors of hell, but that the moderns are most rash and foolish in banishing such beliefs'.[1] Though he lacked the theoretical foundation now available through the sociological and anthropological study of religion, Polybius recognized the power of religious convictions to mold a society.

In the first century CE an unidentified author composed a homily that ultimately entered the New Testament canon as the Epistle to the Hebrews.[2] The lengthy, middle portion of that document (Heb. 7.1–10.18; identified henceforth as the cultic section of Hebrews) includes a critique of the levitical system (the sacrificial cult defined primarily, though not exclusively, in Leviticus). In that critique the author argued that Jesus' death had accomplished, once for all, that purpose for which the levitical system had proven ineffective.[3] From Polybius's perspective, such a fundamental alteration of religious conviction should be

---

1. Polybius, *The Histories* 6.56.6-7, 12. Unless otherwise indicated, all quotations from Josephus, Philo, and from Greco-Roman authors are from the Loeb Classical Library.

2. Henceforth, the individual responsible for the composition of Hebrews will be referred to as the author. Because of the masculine participle in Heb. 11.32, suggesting that the author was a man, masculine pronouns will be employed to refer to the author.

3. Specification of the purpose of the levitical system, as viewed by the author, must be postponed until the detailed examination of the critique is presented.

reflected in the character of the new society in which the recipients of Hebrews were expected to live. The purpose of the research presented here is to analyze the critique of the levitical system in the Epistle to the Hebrews in order to assess the sociological function of that critique. As will be shown, the results of the analysis provide insight into the type of society implied by the author's critique, and into how that implied, ideal society differed from first-century CE hellenistic Judaism, the society from which the recipients of Hebrews came.[4]

The conceptual tools required to pursue this investigation were not available until the 1970s. Nineteen centuries after the composition of Hebrews, New Testament scholars turned to the social sciences seeking new tools with which to illuminate the function and meaning of the canonical texts. Such sociological approaches to the study of these ancient texts can demonstrate how the world described by the various documents reflected the larger society into which Christianity emerged and how the authors sought to define Christian society as a distinct subset of the Greco-Roman world.[5]

A milestone in the sociological study of the New Testament was the working paper by Jonathan Z. Smith on 'The Social Description of Early Christianity'.[6] In that paper, Smith identified four levels of sociological inquiry: '*description of the social facts* given in early Christian materials', 'genuine *social history* of early Christianity', 'the *social organization* of early Christianity in terms of both the *social forces* which led to the rise of Christianity and the *social institutions* of early Christianity', and 'early Christianity as a *social world*, as the creation of a world of meaning which provided a plausibility structure for those who chose to inhabit it' (emphasis original).[7]

---

4. The identification of the author and recipients of Hebrews as Christians with a hellenistic Jewish background will be assumed in the present study. The commentaries on Hebrews listed in the bibliography include discussions of the background of the author and recipients.

5. For a survey of the application of the social sciences to the study of the New Testament, see John Hall Elliot, *What is Social Scientific Criticism?* (Guides to Biblical Scholarship, New Testament Series; Minneapolis: Fortress Press, 1993).

6. Jonathan Z. Smith, 'The Social Description of Early Christianity', *RelSRev* 1 (September 1975), pp. 19-25. Smith presented the paper at the 1973 organizing meeting of the study group on 'The Social World of Early Christianity', a group sponsored jointly by the American Academy of Religion and the Society of Biblical Literature.

7. Smith, 'Social Description', pp. 19-21.

Among the approaches cited by Smith as an example of the fourth category of sociological inquiry was the work of Mary Douglas. In *Natural Symbols*, Douglas developed a paradigm relating the character of a society to the cosmology of that society.[8] Specifically, she sought to understand the function of ritual within a society, and why some societies reject ritual.[9] This paradigm provides a conceptual model with which to seek an answer to the question at hand: what is the sociological function of the critique of the levitical system in the Epistle to the Hebrews?

The State of Research on the Cultic Section of Hebrews

For the first three quarters of the twentieth century Protestant scholars neglected the cultic section of Hebrews. Although several commentaries on the entire epistle were published, a literature review conducted by William Johnsson in 1977 uncovered 'no significant Protestant treatment of this portion of Hebrews [7.1–10.18] in the twentieth century…no monograph has appeared'.[10] Catholic scholars demonstrated greater interest in the cultic section of the epistle, though their primary attention was focussed on questions of 'the ritual of priesthood, often accompanied by a concern to find references to the Mass'.[11]

Since Johnsson's review the deficiency he noted has been addressed partially. Seven dissertations have been completed in which the cultic section of Hebrews was at the heart of the research.[12] Despite this

8. Mary Douglas, *Natural Symbols: Explorations in Cosmology* (New York: Pantheon Books, 3rd. edn, 1982). The first edition was published in 1970.

9. Douglas, *Natural Symbols*, pp. 1, 14.

10. William George Johnsson, 'The Cultus of Hebrews in Twentieth-Century Scholarship', *ExpTim* 89 (January 1978), pp. 104-108.

11. Johnsson, 'The Cultus of Hebrews', p. 104.

12. James A. Young, 'The Significance of Sacrifice in the Epistle to the Hebrews' (ThD dissertation, Southwestern Baptist Theological Seminary, 1963); William George Johnsson, 'Defilement and Purgation in the Book of Hebrews' (PhD dissertation, Vanderbilt University, 1973); Susanne Lehne, *The New Covenant in Hebrews* (JSNTSup, 44; Sheffield: JSOT Press, 1990); John M. Scholer, *Proleptic Priests: Priesthood in the Epistle to the Hebrews* (JSNTSup, 49; Sheffield: JSOT Press, 1991); James Patrick Scullion, 'A Traditio-Historical Study of the Day of Atonement' (PhD dissertation, Catholic University of America, 1991); John Dunnill, *Covenant and Sacrifice in the Letter to the Hebrews* (SNTSMS;

increased interest, none of the studies addressed explicitly the sociological function of the critique of the levitical system. More limited
studies of the cultic section of Hebrews have been published in various
journals and anthologies,[13] but again no one has addressed the specific
question raised in the present research.

David Arthur deSilva has applied sociological insights to the study of
Hebrews,[14] but his work does not resolve the question of the sociological function of the critique of the levitical system. Four reasons can be
cited for this lack of resolution. First, the sociological paradigms employed by deSilva (honor–shame and patron–client) do not exhaust the
possibilities of sociological inquiry nor are they the most obvious
choices for a study of the critique of the levitical system. Second,
deSilva's conclusion on the character of the ideal society implied in
Hebrews conflicts with the conclusion reached by Harold Attridge, the
latter having examined the rhetorical function of the epistle.[15] Third,
deSilva demonstrated reductionistic tendencies when he subordinated
concepts of holiness and of sacrifice to the Greco-Roman institution of

Cambridge: Cambridge University Press, 1992); Darrell Jeffrey Pursiful, *The Cultic
Motif in the Spirituality of the Book of Hebrews* (Lewiston, NY: Mellen Biblical
Press, 1993). Apparently Johnsson limited his search to published monographs, thus
excluding his own dissertation and that of Young.

13. E.g., Harold W. Attridge, 'The Uses of Antithesis in Hebrews 8–10', *HTR*
79 (1986), pp. 1-9; Robert P. Gordon, 'Better Promises: Two Passages in Hebrews
against the Background of the Old Testament Cultus', in William Horbury (ed.),
Templum Amicitiae: Essays on the Second Temple Presented to Ernst Bummel
(Sheffield: Sheffield Academic Press, 1991), pp. 434-49; Kenneth Grayston,
'Salvation Proclaimed III. Hebrews 9[11-14]', *ExpTim* 93 (1982), pp. 164-68; James
Swetnam, 'Christology and the Eucharist in the Epistle to the Hebrews', *Bib* 70
(1989), pp. 74-95; Albert Vanhoye, 'Esprit éternel et feu du sacrifice en He 9,14',
Bib 64 (1983), pp. 263-74.

14. David Arthur deSilva, 'Despising Shame: A Cultural-Anthropological
Investigation of the Epistle to the Hebrews', *JBL* 113 (1994), pp. 439-61; *idem*,
'The Epistle to the Hebrews in Social-Scientific Perspective', *ResQ* 36 (1994),
pp. 1-21; *idem, Despising Shame: Honor Discourse and Community Maintenance
in the Epistle to the Hebrews* (SBLDS; Atlanta: Scholars Press, 1995); *idem*,
'Exchanging Favor for Wrath: Apostasy in Hebrews and Patron Client Relationships', *JBL* 115 (1996), pp. 91-116.

15. deSilva, 'Hebrews in Social-Scientific Perspective', pp. 1-21; Harold W.
Attridge, 'Paraenesis in a Homily (λόγος παρακλήσεως): The Possible Location of,
and Socialization in, the "Epistle to the Hebrews" ', *Semeia* 50 (1990), pp. 211-26.

patronage.[16] Finally, Bruce Malina has challenged the methodological foundation of deSilva's major work.[17] In summary, deSilva has not provided a conclusive, convincing answer to the question raised in the present investigation.

One further consideration demonstrates the potential value of an examination of the sociological function of the critique of the levitical system in the Epistle to the Hebrews. In the introduction to his commentary, William Lane noted the lack of consensus on the background and purpose of Hebrews.[18] An examination of various conclusions on the crisis to which the epistle is a reaction and the subsequent response of the author (Table 1) confirms Lane's diagnosis. The length of the cultic section of Hebrews, the central position of that section in the epistle, and the intricate homiletical structure of Hebrews[19] suggest that a determination of the sociological function of the critique of the levitical system may contribute to a resolution of the purpose of the epistle.

Given the current state of research on the Epistle to the Hebrews, further study is warranted. The lack of a sociological examination of the cultic section of the epistle, the limitations of the extant sociological studies of Hebrews, and the absence of a consensus on the background of Hebrews confirm the validity of the present study.

Mary Douglas's Group/Grid Paradigm

Description of the Paradigm
Douglas classified societies according to two parameters: group ('the experience of a bounded social unit') and grid ('rules which relate one person to others on an ego-centered basis').[20] A particular society can be classified as either strong or weak with respect to both group and grid. Four classes of society are defined by this typology (figure 1). Based on anthropological studies of a wide variety of societies, Douglas determined that societies with similar group/grid characteristics tend to have similar cosmologies. For example, similar societies tend to have

---

16. deSilva, 'Exchanging Favor for Wrath', p. 100.
17. Bruce J. Malina, review of *Despising Shame: Honor Discourse and Community Maintenance in the Epistle to the Hebrews* (SBLDS, Atlanta: Scholars Press, 1995), by David Arthur deSilva, in *JBL* 116 (1997), pp. 378-79.
18. William L. Lane, *Hebrews 1–8* (WBC; Dallas: Word Books, 1991), p. xlvii.
19. Lane, *Hebrews 1–8*, pp. lxxxiv-xcviii.
20. Douglas, *Natural Symbols*, p. viii.

Table 1. *Selected proposals for the background of Hebrew*

Crisis	Response
----------------------- Crisis Centered in a Return to Judaism -----------------------	
Dunnill, *Covenant and Sacrifice* (pp. 22, 24, 37) Jewish Christian churches in Asia Minor, facing persecution and disillusionment, members under pressure to return to Judaism	reassure recipients of membership in the household of God
Lehne, *New Covenant* (pp. 16-17, 119) Christians, possibly with dual allegiance (synagogue and church), sensing a lack of cultic observance, nostalgia for Jewish heritage and lack of enthusiasm	depict Christ as the perfect fulfillment of the cultic heritage of Israel and as the superior replacement of that heritage
Ellingworth, *Commentary* (pp. 27, 29, 80) Jewish-Christian congregation considering rejecting or denying Christian distinctives	warn of permanent consequences of rejection and present Christ as the culmination of God's purpose
Lane, *Hebrews 1-8* (pp, liii-liv, lvii, c) Hellenistic Jewish-Christian house church in/near Rome facing Neronian persecution, considering renunciation of commitment to Christ	encourage believers facing persecution, exhort to faithfulness, warn of divine judgment if recipients renounce Christ
Lindars, *Theology* (pp. 7-15) a dissident group within the congregation troubled over the problem of forgiveness for post-baptismal sin, feeling greater benefit from the synagogue, having lost confidence in the Christian assembly	convince the readers that Christ's sacrifice was sufficient in the past and remains effective for all time, inspire confidence in the Christian liturgy
Spicq, *L'épître* (pp. 5-6, 226, 239), *'L'épître'* (p. 390) priests in Jerusalem, some of whom were former Qumran sectarians, sensing attraction to temple cult, ostracized and persecuted by former colleagues, considering renunciation of Christian commitment	exhort the recipients to focus their attention on God's Word and to persevere in the life of faith

Bruce, *Epistle to the Hebrews* (pp. 8-9)
Hellenistic Jewish Christians with a non-conformist background whose spiritual development has been arrested, reluctant to sever ties with a religion recognized by the Romans, inclined to come to a halt or to regress in their spiritual progress

warn against falling back, encouraging recipients that they have everything to gain from faithfulness but everything to lose if they fail

---------------------- Crisis Centered in a Lack of Commitment ----------------------

Attridge, *Hebrews* (p. 13)
persecution and waning commitment to the community's confessed faith

exhortation to faithfulness and deeper understanding to promote covenant fidelity

Moffatt, *Hebrews* (pp. xxiv, xxvi)
not a return to Judaism, but a relaxed commitment to Christianity, failure to recognize that Christianity is the absolute religion

demonstrate from the LXX that the Christian faith alone fulfills the conditions of a real religion

---------------- Crisis Centered in a Challenge to World Mission ----------------

Manson, *Epistle to the Hebrews* (pp. 24, 160)
not a renunciation of Christianity, but a conservative minority within the church, living as Jews, advocating positions similar to the conservative faction in Jerusalem, counter to the world mission of the church

from a position similar to that of Stephen, employ theological and rhetorical skills to demonstrate the necessity of the world mission

Glaze, *No Easy Salvation* (pp. 23-24)
Jewish Christian majority in a synagogue compromising their faith out of deference to non-Christian minority in the synagogue, majority unwilling to pay the price of full identification with Christ

challenge the Christian majority to move into the mainstream of world evangelism

------------------------------------ Other Proposals ------------------------------------

Buchanan, *To the Hebrews* (pp. 256, 266-67)

strict sectarian group waiting in Jerusalem for the fulfillment of divine promises to Abraham, doubting the sufficiency of Jesus' self-sacrifice, discouraged and considering departure from Jerusalem	persuade the recipients to hold fast and reassure them that Jesus' self-sacrifice was the perfect gift to motivate God to fulfill promises

Jewett, *Letter to Pilgrims* (pp. 6-13)

written by Epaphras to churches in the Lycus Valley, sent at approximately the same time as Colossians, confronting the same Jewish-Gnostic heresy being addressed in Colossians	counter the gnostic teaching, exhort the recipients to join in the pilgrim journey in encounter with God, and depict Christ as sharing in the hardships of pilgrimage

similar attitudes toward purity, the purpose and efficacy of ritual, and the personification of the cosmos.[21]

Response to ritual was a central concern in Douglas's work. The thesis presented and defended in *Natural Symbols* was:

> the most important determinant of ritualism is the experience of closed social groups. The man who has that experience associates boundaries with power and danger. The better defined and the more significant the social boundaries, the more the bias I would expect in favor of ritual. If the social groups are weakly structured and their membership weak and fluctuating, then I would expect low value to be set on symbolic performance. Along this line of ritual variation appropriate doctrinal differences would appear. With weak social boundaries and weak ritualism, I would expect doctrinal emphasis on internal, emotional states. Sin would be more a matter of affect than of transgression; sacraments and magic would give way to direct, unmediated communion, even to the sacralisation of states of trance and bodily dissociation.[22]

In her subsequent development of the paradigm, Douglas broadened the scope of the model in an attempt to relate 'certain distinctive values and belief systems' to 'the legitimation of actions taken'.[23] This expansion of scope did not negate the applicability of group/grid analysis to questions of ritualism.

21. Douglas, *Natural Symbols*, p. 105.
22. Douglas, *Natural Symbols*, p. 14.
23. Mary Douglas, 'Cultural Bias', in Mary Douglas, *In the Active Voice* (London: Routledge and Kegan Paul, 1982), pp. 183-254 (247).

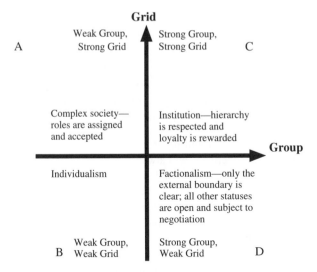

Figure 1. *Group/grid quadrants. Adapted from Mary Douglas,* Natural Symbols, *p. 59, and Howard Clark Kee,* Knowing the Truth: A Sociological Approach to New Testament Interpretation, *p. 16.*

Since Douglas's initial presentation, other authors have offered comments on and modifications to the paradigm.[24] Sheldon Isenberg and Dennis Owen identified nine parameters by which the four characteristic cosmologies can be described (table 2). Jonathan Gross and Steve Rayner proposed a set of 'predicates' (five for group and four for grid) that can be employed for objective determination of group and grid.[25] As with Douglas's later work, the modifications proposed by other authors refined and broadened the model without negating the value of group/grid analysis in studies of response to ritual.

Applicability of the Paradigm in the Present Research
Assessment of the applicability of group/grid analysis to a study of the sociological function of the critique of the levitical system in the Epistle to the Hebrews begins with the inherent attributes of the model. The most important consideration is the commensurability of the model

24. Sheldon R. Isenberg and Dennis E. Owen, 'Bodies, Natural and Contrived: The Work of Mary Douglas', *RelSRev* 3 (1977), pp. 1-17; Jonathan L. Gross and Steve Rayner, *Measuring Culture: A Paradigm for the Analysis of Social Organization* (New York: Columbia University Press, 1985); Mary Douglas (ed.), *Essays in the Sociology of Perception* (London: Routledge and Kegan Paul, 1982).
25. Gross and Rayner, *Measuring Culture*, pp. 71-85.

with the research problem. Group/grid analysis is a social-scientific tool incorporating consideration of the attitude toward ritual. The critique of the levitical system in Hebrews is a response to a particular ritual; therefore, group/grid analysis is a reasonable choice for an analytical tool with which to address the sociological function of the critique.

Douglas developed group/grid analysis as a comparative tool.[26] The range over which legitimate comparisons may be made is limited:

> The hypothesis which I will propose about concordance between symbolic and social experience will always have to be tested within a given social environment... The latitude allowed by the term 'given social environment' is a matter of discretion. It does not allow me to claim that the comparison of Congo net hunters with Arizona sheep herders validates my thesis. Only if various pygmy bands, net hunters and archers and their neighboring Bantu farmers were compared would the conclusions be interesting. The more limited the cultural ranges within which the comparison is made, the more significant the results.[27]

First-century CE hellenistic Judaism is the natural choice for the society with which to compare the ideal society implied by the author of Hebrews. The author and recipients were former members of hellenistic Jewish society, and, as residents of the Roman Empire, the author and recipients would have continued to interact with hellenistic Jews. Further, the levitical system critiqued by the author was an integral component of first-century CE Judaism; therefore, first-century CE hellenistic Judaism is the most natural choice for a society with which to compare the author's ideal society.

One potential obstacle to the application of group/grid analysis in New Testament scholarship is the nature of the available data. Douglas based her work on examinations of contemporary societies and, in their refinement of the model, Gross and Rayner assumed that the researcher has direct access to the subject societies. In the application of sociological research to the study of the New Testament, as with any sociological analysis of an ancient society, the researcher has no direct access to the subject societies; questions for which the extant artifacts provide no relevant data may be unanswerable. One consequence of this limitation is that the objective predicates proposed by Gross and Rayner are not directly applicable to New Testament studies.

---

26. Douglas, *Natural Symbols*, p. 64; *idem*, 'The Background of the Grid Dimension: A Comment', *Sociological Analysis* 50 (1989), pp. 171-76 (174).

27. Douglas, *Natural Symbols*, p. 64.

Table 2. Descriptions of the characteristic group/grid cosmologies

	A.\nWeak Group, Strong Grid	C.\nStrong Group, Strong Grid	B.\nWeak Group, Weak Grid	D.\nStrong Group, Weak Grid
Purity	pragmatic attitude, pollution not automatic; bodily waste not threatening, may be recycled	strong concern for purity; well-defined purification rituals; purity rules define and maintain social structure	rejected; anti-purity	strong concern for purity but inside of the social and physical bodies are under attack; pollution present and purification ritual ineffective
Ritual	will be used for private ends if present; ego remains superior; condensed symbols do not delimit reality	a ritualistic society; ritual expresses the internal classification system	rejected; anti-ritual; effervescent; spontaneity valued	ritualistic; ritual focused upon group boundaries, concerned with expelling pollutants (witches) from social body
Magic	private; may be a strategy for success	belief in the efficacy of symbolic behavior	none; magic rejected	ineffective in protecting individual and social bodies; a source of danger and pollution
Personal Identity	pragmatic and adaptable	a matter of internalizing clearly articulated social roles; individual subservient to but not in conflict with society	no antagonism between society and self but old society may be seen as oppressive; roles rejected, self-control and social control low	located in group membership, not in the internalization of roles, which are confused; distinction between appearance and internal state

Body	instrumental; self-controlled; pragmatic attitude	tightly controlled but a symbol of life	irrelevant; life is spiritual; purity concerns absent but body may be rejected; may be used freely or asceticism may prevail	social and physical bodies tightly controlled but under attack; invaders have broken through bodily boundaries; not a symbol of life
Trance	not dangerous	dangerous; either not allowed or tightly controlled and limited to a group of experts	approved, even welcomed; no fear of loss of self-control	dangerous; a matter of demonic possession; evil
Sin	failure; loss of face; stupidity	the violation of formal rules; focus upon behavior instead of internal state of being; ritual (magic) efficacious in counteracting sin	a matter of ethics and interiority	a matter of pollution; evil lodged within person and society; sin much like a disease; internal state of being more important than adherence to formal rules, but the latter still valued
Personification of the Cosmos	geared to individual success and initiative; cosmos is benignly amoral; God as junior partner	anthropomorphic; non-dualistic; the universe is just and non-capricious	likely to be impersonal; individual access, usually direct; no mediation; benign	anthropomorphic; dualistic; warring forces of good and evil; universe is not just and may be whimsical
Suffering and Misfortune	an intelligent person ought to be able to avoid them	the result of automatic punishment for the violation of formal rules; part of the divine economy	love conquers all	unjust; not automatic punishment; attributed to malevolent forces

Source: Sheldon R. Isenberg and Dennis E. Owen, 'Bodies, Natural and Contrived: The Work of Mary Douglas', *RelSRev* 3 (1977), pp. 7-8.

Despite this limitation, group/grid analysis may be employed caut-
iously in New Testament scholarship. Though the detailed data required
by Gross and Rayner are not available, evidence of the strength of
group identity and of internal structure and regulation (i.e. grid) are
present in the literary and archaeological artifacts. The writings of Philo
and Josephus allow the researcher to gain insight into first-century CE
hellenistic Judaism, and these insights can be corroborated by the
writings of Greco-Roman authors, by New Testament descriptions of
first-century Judaism, and by the examination of the remains of Jewish
synagogues and tombs. Because of the inability to identify precisely the
location of the recipients of Hebrews or the location from which the
epistle was sent, no archeological data are available for a description of
the ideal society. If the locations could be determined accurately and
precisely, the archeological data would be of uncertain value, for the
response of the recipients to the author's exhortation is unknown.
Consequently, the text of Hebrews is the only available set of data on
the author's implied ideal society.

Because the present research depends heavily on literary data, the
cautions expressed by Richard Rohrbaugh are relevant. He noted that (1)
literary evidence must not be confused for the 'common sense...every-
day experience' of living in a society, particularly when all of the extant
literature was composed by a single individual; (2) individuals might be
members of multiple overlapping social groups; and (3) the character of
a social group is defined by both internal and external pressures.[28]

Three considerations limit the negative impact on the present research
of Rohrbaugh's comments. First, the primary subject under study is not
the actual society in which the author or recipients lived but the ideal
society advocated implicitly by the author; therefore, his implicit
characterization of that ideal society is definitive. Second, consideration
of the other social groups of which the recipients were members would
be relevant to an assessment of the recipients' response to the epistle,
but such a concern is beyond the scope of the present study. Conversely, from the perspective of the author, identification of the other
groups of which he was a member would be necessary to explain why
he envisioned this particular ideal society, but, again, such a concern is
beyond the scope of the present study. Third, the primary external
pressures were the influences upon the recipients of first-century CE

28. Richard L. Rohrbaugh, "Social Location of Thought' as a Heuristic Construct in New Testament Study' *JSNT* 30 (1987), pp. 103-109 (108-109).

hellenistic Judaism and of the larger Greco-Roman world. Judaism was the society with which the author contrasted his ideal society, and this external pressure is addressed in the present study. Romans did not distinguish sharply between Jews and Christians until the localized persecution by Nero (i.e., not earlier than 64 CE), and even as late as the end of the first century CE Christians were viewed by some Romans as a subset of Judaism.[29] Consequently, early Roman references to Christians are ambiguous, and cannot be associated definitively with the author or recipients of Hebrews. The only clear evidence of external pressures on the recipients of Hebrews are the references to past (Heb. 10.32-34) and anticipated (Heb. 12.3-4) afflictions; these comments will be addressed in detail below. Although Rohrbaugh's caveats do not invalidate the present investigation, they do serve a cautionary function, limiting the conclusions that may be drawn from a sociological analysis of Hebrews.

Conclusion

The conclusion presented in the present study is that the critique of the levitical system in Hebrews functions sociologically by supporting the author's implicit advocacy of an ideal society. Further, that ideal society was both more open to outsiders and more willing to assimilate fully new members than was first-century CE hellenistic Judaism. The argument involves:

1. demonstrating that first-century Judaism was a strong group, strong grid society within the larger Greco-Roman world,
2. confirming that the ideal society was weaker in terms of both group and grid than first-century Judaism,
3. verifying that the critique of the levitical system in Hebrews is a component of a coherent weak group, weak grid cosmology, and
4. relating the critique of the levitical system to the overall purpose of the epistle.

29. Suetonius, *Claudius* 25.4; *idem, Domitian* 12.4. In comments on the text of his translation of the latter citation, J.C. Rolfe interpreted the reference to those who lived as Jews without acknowledging that faith as a description of 'Christians, whom the Romans commonly confounded with the Jews'; Suetonius, *Domitian*, in *The Lives of the Caesars* (trans. J.C. Rolfe; LCL; Cambridge; Harvard University Press; London: William Heinemann, 1914), p. 366.

In the remainder of this study, the implicitly described ideal society will be referred to simply as the 'implied society'. The status of that society as the author's ideal construct, not an actual functioning society, should be understood.

Chapter 2

GROUP/GRID ANALYSIS OF FIRST-CENTURY CE
HELLENISTIC JUDAISM

Jewish society in the first century CE existed within the larger matrix of Greco-Roman society. Assessment of the group/grid status of first-century CE hellenistic Judaism requires a determination of the situation of the Jewish people within that larger society. Two major data sources are available: the writings of Josephus and of Philo. These authors represent complementary viewpoints, Josephus being a resident of the Jewish homeland while Philo was a son of the Diaspora. Both Josephus and Philo participated in delegations to Rome, and Josephus spent the final years of his life in the imperial capital; therefore, both can be assumed to be familiar with the larger Jewish community in the Roman Empire.

The greatest shortcoming in depending on Josephus and Philo is that neither may be assumed to represent the less educated, less affluent, less influential members of Jewish society. This weakness is common to all studies dependant on ancient literary sources. Literacy was most common among the educated, affluent, and influential segments of ancient society; consequently, such individuals were most likely to leave literary works to be discovered by later generations.

Incorporating other data sources can minimize the negative consequences of the dependence on Jewish aristocrats. Though their perspective was often lacking in objectivity, Greco-Roman authors were familiar with some of the distinguishing characteristics of Jewish society. By comparing and contrasting the comments of Philo and of Josephus with the observations of Greco-Roman authors, a skeletal description of first-century CE hellenistic Judaism can be composed. Data supporting such a description may be gleaned from the New Testament. Paul (an 'anomalous' diaspora Jew[1]) and the author of Luke–Acts (usually,

1. John M.G. Barclay, *Jews in the Mediterranean Diaspora: From Alexander to Trajan (323 BCE–117 CE)* (Edinburgh: T. & T. Clark, 1996), p. 381. Because of

though not unanimously, identified as a gentile, perhaps a God-fearer[2]) represent a perspective poised between the Jewish and gentile worlds. Their references to distinctive Jewish practices and beliefs can be employed to supplement Jewish and Greco-Roman sources. In the following discussion selected New Testament texts and Greco-Roman authors from the first century BCE through the second century CE will be cited to confirm the assertions of Philo and Josephus.[3]

Group status of first-century CE hellenistic Judaism can be established by identifying the boundary that divided Jews from gentiles. The number of boundary markers and the importance attached to those markers provides a means of assessing the strength of group identity. In this phase of the study, the use of Jewish, New Testament, and Greco-Roman sources will be particularly valuable, allowing the boundary to be viewed from multiple perspectives.

> The term grid suggests the cross-hatch of rules to which individuals are subject in the course of their interaction. As a dimension, it shows a progressive change in the mode of control. At the strong end there are visible rules about space and time related to social roles; at the other end, near zero, the formal classifications fade, and finally vanish.[4]

Assessment of the grid status of first-century CE hellenistic Judaism involves, therefore, a determination of the degree to which the lives of first-century Jews were regulated. The same sources employed in

questions about the authorship of some of the documents comprising the canonical Pauline corpus, only the seven generally accepted epistles (Rom., 1 Cor., 2 Cor., Gal., Phil., 1 Thess. and Phil.) are emphasized in the following discussion.

2.   Darrell L. Bock, *Luke 1:1–9:50* (Baker Exegetical Commentary on the New Testament; Grand Rapids: Baker Book House, 1994), pp. 6-7; Joseph A. Fitzmeyer, *The Gospel According to Luke (I–IX)* (AB; Garden City, NY: Doubleday, 1981), p. 42; John Nolland, *Luke 1–9:20* (WBC; Dallas: Word Books, 1989), pp. xxxii, xxxix; John B. Polhill, *Acts* (The New American Commentary; Nashville: Broadman Press, 1992), p. 27.

3.   Dio Cassius (c. 150–235) and Philostratus (c. 170–c. 245 CE) represent exceptions to the restriction of Greco-Roman sources to the range of first century BCE to second century CE. Dio Cassius's *Roman History* was included because of its value as a history of the early empire. Inclusion of Philostratus's work, *The Life of Apollonius of Tyana*, was based on the fact that Philostratus was presenting a biography of a first-century CE philosopher. Because of the uncertain authenticity of the comments attributed to Apollonius by Philostratus, less weight should be attached to this source than to the others cited.

4.   Douglas, 'Cultural Bias', p. 192.

assessing group status will be used in the assessment of grid status. Gross and Rayner identified four predicates for measuring grid:

1. specialization—narrowness in the assignment of roles, especially high-status roles
2. asymmetry—lack of symmetry in role exchanges among members
3. entitlement—assignment of roles by ascription rather than by achievement
4. accountability—imposition of sanctions by those in dominant roles against those in subordinate roles[5]

Although the nature of the available data preclude the objective, quantitative calculations proposed by Gross and Rayner, their predicates provide guidance in assessing grid.

Group Characteristics of Hellenistic Judaism

References to diverse populations as 'Jew and Greek' or 'Jew and gentile', present both in Paul's epistles (Rom. 1.16; 3.29; 9.24; 1 Cor. 12.13; Gal. 2.14; 3.28) and in Luke–Acts (Acts 14.1, 5; 18.4; 19.10, 17; 20.21), constitute evidence that Jews in the first century CE possessed a clear group identity. Characteristics defining that identity can be discerned in Tacitus's introduction to his account of the destruction of Jerusalem, where the historian presented a portrait of the Jewish people.

> To establish his influence over this people for all time, Moses introduced new religious practices, quite opposed to those of all other religions. The Jews regard as profane all that we hold sacred; on the other hand, they permit all that we abhor... They abstain from pork, in recollection of a plague, for the scab to which this animal is subject once afflicted them. By frequent fasts even now they bear witness to the long hunger with which they were once distressed, and the unleavened Jewish bread is still employed in memory of the haste with which they seized the grain. They say that they first chose to rest on the seventh day because that day ended their toils; but after a time they were led by the charms of indolence to give over the seventh year as well to inactivity.
>
> Whatever their origin, these rites are maintained by their antiquity: the other customs of the Jews are base and abominable, and owe their persistence to their depravity. For the worst rascals among other peoples, renouncing their ancestral religions, always kept sending tribute and contributions to Jerusalem, thereby increasing the wealth of the Jews;

---

5.   Gross and Rayner, *Measuring Culture*, pp. 79-82.

again the Jews are extremely loyal toward one another, and always ready to show compassion, but toward every other people they feel only hate and enmity. They sit apart at meals, and they sleep apart, and although as a race, they are prone to lust, they abstain from intercourse with foreign women; yet among themselves nothing is unlawful. They adopted circumcision to distinguish themselves from other peoples by this difference. Those who are converted to their ways follow the same practice, and the earliest lesson they receive is to despise the gods, to disown their country, and to regard their parents, children, and brothers as of little account... The Egyptians worship many animals and monstrous images; the Jews conceive of one god only, and that with the mind alone: they regard as impious those who make from perishable materials representations of gods in man's image; that supreme and eternal being is to them incapable of representation and without end. Therefore they set up no statues in their cities, still less in their temples; this flattery is not paid their kings, nor this honor given to the Caesars. But since their priests used to chant to the accompaniment of pipes and cymbals and to wear garlands of ivy, and because a golden vine was found in their temple, some have thought that they were devotees of Father Liber, the conqueror of the East, in spite of the incongruity of their customs. For Liber established festive rites of a joyous nature, while the ways of the Jews are preposterous and mean.

A great part of Judea is covered with scattered villages, but there are some towns also; Jerusalem is the capital of the Jews. In it was a temple possessing enormous riches. The first line of fortifications protected the city, the next the palace, and the innermost wall the temple. Only a Jew might approach its doors, and all save the priests were forbidden to cross the threshold.

The first Roman to subdue the Jews and set foot in their temple by right of conquest was Gnaeus Pompey: thereafter it was a matter of common knowledge that there were no representations of the gods within, but that the place was empty and the secret shrine contained nothing... Then when Caligula ordered the Jews to set up his statue in their temple, they chose rather to resort to arms, but the emperor's death put an end to their uprising.

The temple was built like a citadel, with walls of its own, which were constructed with more care and effort than any of the rest; the very colonnades about the temple made a splendid defence. Within the enclosure is an ever-flowing spring; in the hills are subterraneous excavations, with pools and cisterns for holding rain-water. The founders of the city had foreseen that there would be many wars because the ways of their people differed so from those of the neighbours.[6]

6.   Tacitus, *Histories* 5.4-5, 8-9, 12.

Between summary statements, declaring that Jews differed profoundly
from their neighbors, the Roman historian offered a catalogue of
boundary markers: the law of Moses, dietary regulations, fasts and festivals (implied in the reference to unleavened bread), Sabbath observance, the sociological consequences of conversion, the temple tax,
refusal of table fellowship with foreigners, endogamy, circumcision,
aniconic monotheism, and the sanctity of the temple. Modern scholarship, attempting to specify the characteristic elements of Jewish identity
within the larger Greco-Roman world, has noted the same distinctives
mentioned by Tacitus;[7] therefore, this catalogue represents a basis for
the consideration of the group characteristics of hellenistic Judaism. In
the following discussion, the goal is not to provide a comprehensive
account of Jewish identity in the first century CE, but to demonstrate
that the Jews constituted a distinctive, well-defined group within Greco-
Roman society.

Aniconic Monotheism
Josephus and Philo concurred on the propriety of a single temple for the
one and only God. The former's aphorism, Εἷς ναὸς ἑνὸς θεοῦ, 'One
temple for the one God'.[8] is in harmony with the more explicit statement by the latter, ἐπειδὴ εἷς ἐστιν ὁ θεός, καὶ ἱερὸν ἕν εἶναι μόνον,
'Since God is one, there should be also one temple'.[9] Similarly, the two
authors agreed that God was not to be represented by any icon
fashioned by human hands. Josephus declared: 'No materials, however
costly, are fit to make an image of Him; no art has skill to conceive and
represent it. The like of Him we have never seen, we do not imagine,
and it is impious to conjecture.'[10] After denouncing the error of
polytheistic worshippers of nature, Philo asserted that

7.   Barclay, *Jews in the Mediterranean Diaspora*, pp. 399-444; Lester L.
Grabbe, *Judaism from Cyrus to Hadrian*. II. *The Roman Period* (Minneapolis:
Fortress Press, 1992), pp. 526-45; James D.G. Dunn, *The Partings of the Ways:
Between Christianity and Judaism and their Significance for the Character of
Christianity* (London: SCM Press; Philadelphia: Trinity Press International, 1991),
pp. 18-36; E.P. Sanders, *Judaism: Practice and Belief 63 BCE–66 CE* (London:
SCM Press; Philadelphia: Trinity Press International, 1992), pp. 47-53, 214, 236-
37, 241; N.T. Wright, *Christian Origins and the Question of God*. I. *The New Testament and the People of God* (Minneapolis: Fortress Press, 1992), pp. 215-43.
8.   Josephus, *Apion* 2.193.
9.   Philo, *Spec. Leg.* 1.67.
10.   Josephus, *Apion* 2.191.

their offence is less than that of the others who have given shape to stocks and stones and silver and gold and similar materials each according to their fancy and then filled the habitable world with images and wooden figures and the other works of human hands fashioned by the craftsmanship of painting and sculpture, arts which have wrought great mischief in the life of mankind.[11]

These convictions are echoed in 1 Cor.. Addressing the issue of the consumption of meat that had been part of a pagan sacrifice, Paul affirmed: 'We know that an idol is nothing in the world and that no one is God except one [οὐδεὶς θεὸς εἰ μὴ εἷς]' (1 Cor. 8.4).[12] This overtly monotheistic confession can be presumed reasonably to reflect Paul's Jewish heritage.

In his elaboration of Num. 31.16 Josephus acknowledged the inherent group-defining function of Jewish worship. He quoted the Midianite maidens' request:

'Seeing then,' said the maidens, 'that ye agree to these conditions, and that ye have customs and a mode of life wholly alien to all mankind, insomuch that your food is of a peculiar sort and your drink is distinct from that of other men, it behoves you, if ye would live with us, also to revere our gods; no other proof can there be of that affection which ye declare that ye now have for us and of its continuance in future, save that ye worship the same gods as we. Nor can any man reproach you for venerating the special gods of the country whereto ye are come, above all when our gods are common to all mankind, while yours has no other worshipper.[13]

Diodorus had reached the same conclusion, citing Jewish worship as an example of their 'unsocial [ἀπάνθρωπόν] and intolerant [μισόξενον]

---

11. Philo, *Decalogo* 66.

12. All New Testament quotations are translations by the author, based on *The Greek New Testament* (eds. Barbara Aland, Kurt Aland, Johannes Karavidopolous, Carlo M. Martini and Bruce M. Metzger; Stuttgart: Deutsche Bibelgesellschaft and United Bible Societies, 4th edn, 1993) and *Novum Testamentum Graece* (ed. Barbara Aland, Kurt Aland, Johannes Karavidopolous, Carlo M. Martini and Bruce M. Metzger; Stuttgart: Deutsche Bibelgesellschaft, 27th edn, 1993). The variant in 1 Cor. 8.4 (inserting ἕτερος after θεὸς, present in ℵ2, 𝔐, and in Syriac versions, but not in 𝔓46, ℵ*, A, B, D, and other manuscripts) emphasizes the monotheistic character of the declaration, though this variant is probably a gloss; cf. Gordon D. Fee, *The First Epistle to the Corinthians* (NICNT; Grand Rapids: Eerdmans, 1987), p. 369.

13. Josephus, *Ant.* 4.137-38.

mode of life.'[14] More poetically, Philostratus quoted Apollonius of Tyana as exclaiming:

> The Jews have long been in revolt not only against the Romans, but against humanity; and a race that has made its own life apart and irreconcilable, that cannot share with the rest of mankind in the pleasures of the table nor join in their libations or prayers or sacrifices, are separated from ourselves by a greater gulf than divides us from Susa or Bactra or the more distant Indies.[15]

These evaluations of Jewish religion, coupled with other comments on the novelty of Jewish aniconic monotheism (e.g. Strabo, *Geography* 16.2.35; Juvenal, *Satires* 14.97; Dio Cassius, *Roman History* 37.17.2; 67.14.2), provide confirming evidence for Lester Grabbe's conclusion that, in their response to hellenism, 'the one area where Jews did find themselves at odds with the rest of the Hellenistic world was in the area of religion. They alone of all ethnic groups refused to honor gods, shrines and cults other than their own.'[16]

The Torah as a Central Symbol

Jacob Neusner concluded that the earliest (pre-70 CE) stratum of the Mishnah was influenced profoundly by the priestly materials in the Torah.[17] He explained this dependance as a reflection of the desire to maintain the 'high and inviolable frontiers around Israel' in a fluid, homogenizing world.[18] This boundary-defining function of the Torah is evident beyond the Mishnah; the Torah served as a distinguishing symbol in the hellenistic Diaspora.

Philo claimed that 'the sanctity of our legislation has been a source of wonder not only to the Jews but also to all other nations.'[19] Describing the role of the Torah in Jewish life, he stated that

> all men guard their own customs, but this is especially true of the Jewish nation. Holding that the laws are oracles vouchsafed by God and having

---

14. Diodorus Siculus, *Historical Library* 40.3.4.

15. Philostratus, *The Life of Apollonius of Tyana* 5.33.

16. Lester L. Grabbe, 'Hellenistic Judaism', in Jacob Neusner (ed.), *Judaism in Late Antiquity* II. *Historical Syntheses* (Handbook of Oriental Studies: The Near and Middle East; Leiden: E.J. Brill, 1995), pp. 53-83 (73).

17. Jacob Neusner, *Judaism: The Evidence of the Mishnah* (Atlanta: Scholars Press, 1988), p. 71.

18. Jacob Neusner, *Judaism: The Evidence of the Mishnah*, p. 75.

19. Philo, *Vit. Mos.* 2.25.

been trained in this doctrine from their earliest years, they carry the likeness of the commandments enshrined in their soul. Then as they contemplate their forms thus clearly represented they always think of them with awe.[20]

Josephus was less complimentary of other nations: 'Most men, so far from living in accordance with their own laws, hardly know what they are... But should anyone of our nation be questioned about the laws, he would repeat them all more readily than his own name.'[21]

In a fragment preserved by Augustine, Seneca concurred with Josephus: 'The Jews, however are aware of the origin and meaning of their rites. The greater part of the people go through a ritual not knowing why they do so.'[22] Another fragment from Seneca confirms the close association of the Jewish people with the Torah: 'Meanwhile the customs of this accursed race gained such influence that they are now received throughout all the world. The vanquished have given laws to their victors.'[23] Similarly, Juvenal complained about individuals who, though they 'flout the laws of Rome, they learn and practise and revere the Jewish law, and all that Moses handed down in his secret tome.'[24]

As recorded in Acts, Stephen's accusers affirmed the centrality of the Torah as a defining symbol for Judaism. They charged that 'this man does not cease speaking words against this holy place and the law; for we have heard him saying that this Jesus the Nazarene will destroy this place and will alter the customs that Moses handed down to us' (Acts 6.13-14). Paul included the giving of the law (νομοθεσία; Rom. 9.4) in his inventory of the blessings of Israel and contrasted the status of those under grace (Rom. 6.14, 15), those living by faith (Gal. 3.23), and those led by the Spirit (Gal. 5.18) with the status of those who were ὑπὸ νόμον, 'under the law' (cf. 1 Cor. 9.20, where being a Jew is described in a parallel phrase as being ὑπὸ νόμον).

Three ceremonial acts confirm the symbolic importance of the Torah in Jewish life. Diodorus reported that Antiochus defiled the Jewish holy books (τὰς ἱερὰς αὐτῶν βίβλους) as part of his appropriation of the

20. Philo, *Leg. Gai.* 210-11.

21. Josephus, *Apion* 176, 178. The strength of the contrast is suggested by the emphatic placement of ἡμῶν at the beginning of the sentence in §178.

22. Augustine, *The City of God* 6.11.

23. Augustine, *The City of God* 6.11.

24. Juvenal, *Satires* 14.100-102.

temple.[25] Josephus recounted that the parade of spoils from the destruction of Jerusalem concluded with a Torah scroll (ὅ τε νόμος ὁ τῶν Ἰουδαίων).[26] Finally, Philo described the Alexandrian Jews' annual celebration of the translation of the Septuagint.[27] John M.G. Barclay characterized this feast as

> a celebration unique among the multifarious festivals of the Graeco-Roman world… Never before in the history of religion had a *translation* been the focus of such religious celebration. It was only among the Jews that written documents were accorded such direct revelatory significance, and only among Diaspora Jews, unable to read their original script, that their Greek version could be the object of such respect (emphasis original).[28]

N.T. Wright described the devotion to the Torah among diaspora Jews as 'the focal point of Jewishness. For millions of ordinary Jews, Torah became a portable Land, a movable Temple.'[29] The idea of the Torah as a substitute temple is suggested by the mishnaic discussion associating Torah study with the divine presence (שכינה).[30] Based on the participants identified in the discussion, an estimated date of c. 110 CE can be deduced. At this time all Jews were, in effect, in the Diaspora with respect to the temple cult. The comments of the rabbis might, therefore, reflect a diaspora theology of the Torah that was extant before the destruction of the temple.

James D.G. Dunn stated that 'in sociological terms the law functioned as an 'identity marker' and 'boundary', reinforcing Israel's assumption of distinctiveness and distinguishing Israel from the surrounding nations.'[31] The symbolic import of the Torah, gentile reactions to the Jewish reverence of the Torah, the exaltation of the Torah by Philo and by Josephus, and the influence of the Torah on later developments in Judaism (i.e. the formation of the Mishnah) support Dunn's conclusion.

25. Diodorus Siculus, *Historical Library* 34/35.1.4.
26. Josephus, *War* 7.150.
27. Philo, *Vit. Mos.* 2.41-44.
28. Barclay, *Jews in the Mediterranean Diaspora*, p. 424.
29. Wright, *The New Testament and the People of God*, p. 228.
30. *m. Ab.* 3.2-6.
31. Dunn, *The Partings of the Ways*, p. 26.

The Practice of the Torah

Beyond the symbolic significance of the Torah as scripture, obedience to the requirements of the Torah served to identify Jews as a distinct group within Greco-Roman society. Most prominent among the elements of Torah praxis were sabbath observance, participation in feasts and fasts, circumcision, dietary regulations, and endogamy. These provisions, to which Jews 'generally remained loyal…both in public and in private life,'[32] 'reinforced the sense of distinctive identity and marked Israel off most clearly from other nations.'[33]

Sabbath Observance. In Luke–Acts synagogue attendance on the Sabbath is portrayed as the custom (κατὰ τὸ εἰωθὸς) of Jesus (Lk. 4.16) and of Paul (Acts 17.2).[34] Public reading of the scriptures was assumed to be a regular Sabbath activity (Lk. 4.16-17; Acts 13.27; 15.21). The importance of 'proper' Sabbath observance is evident in Jesus' conflicts with lawyers, scribes, Pharisees, and synagogue officials (Lk. 6.1-11; 13.10-17; 14.1-6).

Philo opened his discussion of the Sabbath commandment by noting the distinctive nature of the weekly observance:

> The fourth commandment deals with the sacred seventh day, that it should be observed in a reverent and religious manner. While some states celebrate this day as a feast once a month, reckoning it from the commencement as shown by the moon, the Jewish nation never ceases to do so at continuous intervals with six days between each.[35]

After contemplating the mystical significance of the number seven, Philo credited Moses with

> inscrib[ing] its beauty on the most holy tables of the Law, and impress[ing] it on the minds of all who were set under him, by bidding them at intervals of six days to keep a seventh day holy, abstaining from other work that has to do with seeking and gaining a livelihood, and

---

32. S. Safrai, 'Relations between the Diaspora and the Land of Israel', in S. Safrai, M. Stern, D. Flusser, and W.C. van Unnik (eds.), *The Jewish People in the First Century: Historical Geography, Political History, Social, Cultural and Religious Life and Institutions* (CRINT; Assen: Van Gorcum, 1974), pp. 154-215 (185).

33. Dunn, *The Partings of the Ways*, p. 28.

34. Cf. the resting of the female disciples on the Sabbath day following the crucifixion, 'according to the commandment [κατὰ τὴν ἐντολήν]' (Lk. 23.56).

35. Philo, *Dec.* 96.

giving their time to the one sole object of philosophy with a view to the improvement of character and submission to the scrutiny of conscience.[36]

Despite his proclivity for allegorizing, Philo rejected explicitly the neglect of the literal observance of the Sabbath rest.[37]

Gentile authors were unimpressed with the benefits and rewards of the Sabbath. Juvenal satirized those 'who have a father who reveres the Sabbath [*sabbata*]', a day devoted to 'idleness'.[38] According to Augustine, Seneca also censured the Sabbath 'because by introducing one day of rest in every seven they lose in idleness almost a seventh of their life, and by failing to act in times of urgency they often suffer loss.'[39] Tacitus concurred, attributing widespread Sabbath observance among the Jews to 'the charms of indolence'.[40] Dio Cassius described Jewish Sabbath activities as 'no serious occupation'.[41] Seneca ridiculed a ritual that marked the beginning of the Sabbath: 'But let us forbid lamps to be lighted on the Sabbath, since the gods do not need light, neither do men take pleasure in soot.'[42]

Because the Sabbath was a 'well-known, and frequently resented... ethnic peculiarity which marked off Jewish communal life from that of all other peoples',[43] official sanction for Sabbath observance was treasured by the Jews. Philo recorded Agrippa's plea to Gaius (Caligula), in which the Jewish ruler reminded the emperor of the Augustan decree permitting the Jews to celebrate the Sabbath.[44] Josephus preserved the text of such a proclamation, exempting Jews from having to appear in court on the Sabbath.[45] A collection of official correspondence, also preserved by Josephus, affirms various distinctive Jewish privileges, including Sabbath observance.[46]

36. Philo, *Op. Mund.* 128.
37. Philo, *Migr. Abr.* 91.
38. Juvenal, *Satires* 14.96, 106.
39. Augustine, *The City of God* 6.11.
40. Tacitus, *Histories* 5.4.
41. Dio Cassius, *Roman History* 37.17.3.
42. Seneca, *Epistulae Morales* 95.47.
43. Barclay, *Jews in the Mediterranean Diaspora*, p. 440. Cf. Dunn, *The Partings of the Ways*, p. 30, 'a badge of ethnic identity and devotion to ancestral custom'; Wright, *The New Testament and the People of God*, p. 238, 'demarcated the covenant people, and...provided litmus tests of covenant loyalty.'
44. Philo, *Leg. Gai.* 311-13.
45. Josephus, *Ant.* 16.163.
46. Josephus, *Ant.* 14.224-64.

Feasts and Fasts. The writings of Josephus, of Philo, and of Paul suggest the importance of the festival calendar in first-century CE hellenistic Judaism. Josephus described the sacrifices offered at Rosh HaShanah, Yom Kippur, Succot (Tabernacles), Passover, and Shavuot (Pentecost), and promised a further discussion (either not completed or no longer extant).[47] Philo devoted most of the second book of *De Specialibus Legibus* to a discussion of the 'ten feasts' of the Jews: every day, Sabbath, new moon, Passover, offering of the sheaf, Unleavened Bread, Shavuot, Rosh HaShanah (called the 'Sacred-month-day' [ἱερομηνία]), Yom Kippur, and Succot.[48] The significance of the festal calendar in Judaism is implicit in Paul's marking of the flow of time according to the feasts (1 Cor. 16.8; cf. Acts 20.16; 27.9) and by his appropriation of Passover as a christological symbol (1 Cor. 5.7-8).

Greco-Roman references to the Jewish feasts and fasts are limited. Tacitus's mention of the 'unleavened Jewish bread'[49] suggests an acquaintance with the practices of Passover. More extensive, though confused, is the account by Plutarch, who conflated Yom Kippur and Succot.[50] Supplementing this scant literary evidence are numerous inscriptions, suggesting that diaspora Jews celebrated the feasts and fasts in a manner similar to the observances in Jerusalem.[51]

Participation in the annual cycle of feasts and fasts strengthened the group identity of diaspora Jews in two ways. Links to Jerusalem were reinforced by festival pilgrimages (cf. the Pentecost account in Acts 2) and by the prerogative of the temple-based priesthood to set the liturgical calendar.[52] The second mechanism for strengthening group identity

---

47. Josephus, *Ant.* 3.239-57.

48. Philo, *Spec. Leg.* 2.41-213; this discussion constitutes 173 of the 262 sections (i.e. almost two-thirds) of book 2.

49. Tacitus, *Histories* 5.4.

50. Plutarch, *Quaestiones Conviviales* 4.6.2.

51. Emil Schürer, *A History of the Jewish People in the Age of Jesus Christ* (4 vols.; trans. and rev. by Geza Vermes, Fergus Millar, Matthew Black and Martin Goodman; Edinburgh: T. & T. Clark, 1986), III, p. 144. Also of note are the symbols incorporated into the Jewish catacomb inscriptions in Rome. Leon associated the frequent *lulav* and *etrog* with Succot and the *shofar* with Rosh HaShanah; Harry Joshua Leon, *The Jews of Ancient Rome* (updated edn, with a new introduction by Carolyn A. Osiek; Peabody, MA: Hendrickson, 1995), pp. 198-200.

52. Safrai, 'Relations between the Diaspora and the Land of Israel', pp. 186, 206-207; *idem*, 'The Temple', in. S. Safrai, M. Stern, D. Flusser and W.C. van Unnik (eds.), *The Jewish People in the First Century: Historical Geography, Polit-*

derives from the sociological function of ritual. Emile Durkheim included in his definition of religion the 'unified system of...*practices* relative to sacred things...*which unite* into one single moral community...all those who adhere to them' (emphasis mine).[53] Joachim Wach stated that 'worship...forms, integrates, and develops the religious group... Prayer, sacrifice, and ritual not only serve to articulate the experiences of those taking part but contribute in no small measure to the shaping and determining of the organization and spirit of the group.'[54] The explicit connections to Jerusalem and the formative power of the festivals worked in concert to contribute to the cementing together of all Jews.

Circumcision. Though circumcision was known to be practiced by other nations,[55] the custom came to be viewed as a distinctive mark of the Jews. Paul's description of the division of labor in the church's missionary effort equated circumcision with Jewish audiences and uncircumcision with gentile audiences (Gal. 2.7-9). Tacitus claimed that 'they adopted circumcision to distinguish themselves from other peoples by this difference.'[56] For Petronius circumcision was as stereotypically Jewish as were the dark skin of the Ethiopians and the pale faces of the Gauls.[57] In a judicial context, Suetonius recalled an instance in which circumcision was adequate evidence to demonstrate that an individual was a Jew.[58] Strabo attributed the Jewish practice of circumcision to superstition.[59]

Aware of gentile ridicule, Philo devoted the opening paragraphs of *De Specialibus Legibus* to a defense of the rite of circumcision.[60] Though he emphasized the symbolic value of the rite, the Alexandrian

ical History, Social, Cultural and Religious Life and Institutions (CRINT; Assen: Van Gorcum, 1974), pp. 865-907 (877, 898-99); Grabbe, *Judaism from Cyrus to Hadrian*, p. 545; *m. Rosh HaSh.* 1:3-4.

53. Emile Durkheim, *Elementary Forms of Religious Life* (trans. Joseph Ward Swain; Glencoe, IL: Free Press, 1954), p. 47.

54. Joachim Wach, *Sociology of Religion* (Chicago: University of Chicago Press, 1944), pp. 39, 40.

55. Diodorus Siculus, *Historical Library* 1.28.2-3.

56. Tacitus, *Histories* 5.5.

57. Petronius, *Satyricon* 102.

58. Suetonius, *Domitian* 12.2.

59. Strabo, *Geography* 16.2.37.

60. Philo, *Spec. Leg.* 1.1-11.

insisted that the literal practice not be neglected.[61] Josephus, likewise aware of the gentile attitude,[62] explained circumcision as a means to ensure the genetic purity of the Jewish nation.[63] In his account of the conversion to Judaism of the royal family of Adiabene, Josephus recorded the opinion that circumcision was a legal prerequisite to being βεβαίως Ἰουδαῖος, 'genuinely a Jew'.[64] These testimonies support strongly the conclusion that 'in the Roman environment...circumcision constituted, for males, a practically unambiguous token of Jewish identity.'[65]

Kashrut and Table Fellowship. A shared meal is a significant social event.

> Meals in antiquity were what anthropologists call 'ceremonies'. Unlike 'rituals', which confirm a change of status, ceremonies are regular, predictable events in which roles and statuses in a community are affirmed or legitimated... Because eating together implied sharing a common set of ideas and values, and frequently a common social position as well, it is important to ask: Who eats with whom?... What does one eat?[66]

For Judaism, such questions are answered in the kashrut laws.

References to kosher dietary rules by hellenistic Jews confirm the practice in the first century CE. Josephus quoted the Midianite maidens' complaint about the idiosyncracy of the Jewish diet, and noted the willingness of the Jews to die rather than violate the kashrut regulations.[67] Philo recorded an incident when Alexandrians confirmed the Jewish identity of women by challenging the suspects to eat pork, and described the ridicule heaped upon the Jewish delegation when the question of eating pork was raised by emperor Gaius.[68]

Kashrut and table fellowship were crucial issues in the early church's self-definition with respect to Judaism. Paul perceived Peter's with-

---

61. Philo, *Migr. Abr.* 92-93.
62. Josephus, *Apion* 2.137.
63. Josephus, *Ant.* 1.192.
64. Josephus, *Ant.* 20.38.
65. Barclay, *Jews in the Mediterranean Diaspora*, p. 438.
66. Bruce J. Malina and Richard L. Rohrbaugh, *Social-Science Commentary on the Synoptic Gospels* (Minneapolis: Fortress Press, 1992), p. 135.
67. Josephus, *Ant.* 4.137; *idem*, *Apion* 2.234.
68. Philo, *Flacc.* 95-96; *idem*, *Leg. Gai.* 361-63.

drawal from table fellowship with gentile believers as a crisis (Gal. 2.11-14). In Luke–Acts transcendence of the kashrut restrictions was employed as a symbol of the church's openness to gentiles (Acts 10.9-48). Despite this annulment, gentile Christians were urged to accommodate the dietary sensitivities of their Jewish brothers and sisters (Acts 15.28-29).

Greco-Roman curiosity over the Jewish kashrut regulations is evident in Plutarch's *Quaestiones Conviviales*, where he presented an extended dialogue on the question, 'Whether the Jews abstain from pork because of reverence or aversion for the pig.'[69] Other gentile authors described the Jewish dietary regulations, and the consequent limits to table fellowship, as outlandish, superstitious, and as an example of the Jewish hatred for and rebellion against all humanity.[70] Such reactions to kashrut support Dunn's conclusion that 'these dietary rules constituted one of the test cases for Jewish identity, *one of the clearest boundary markers which distinguished Jew from Gentile and which were recognized as such*' (emphasis original).[71]

Endogamy. Joseph and Aseneth, a hellenistic-Jewish romance composed between 100 BCE and 100 CE, amplified the biblical account of the marriage of the son of Jacob to the daughter of an Egyptian priest. When Aseneth first attempted to kiss Joseph, the Hebrew rebuffed her, declaring:

> It is not fitting for a man who worships God…to kiss a strange woman… But a man who worships God will kiss his mother and the sister (who is born) of his clan and family and the wife who shares his bed, (all of) who(m) bless with their mouths the living God. Likewise, for a woman who worships God it is not fitting to kiss a strange man, because this is an abomination before the Lord God.[72]

This insistence on endogamy provides the conflict that drives the subsequent plot.[73]

The words of Philo and Josephus confirm that endogamy was not a literary fiction created by the author of *Joseph and Aseneth*, but was

69. Plutarch, *Quaestiones Conviviales* 4.5.

70. Strabo, *Geography* 16.2.37; Diodorus Siculus, *Historical Library* 34/35.1.2; Philostratus, *The Life of Apollonius of Tyana* 5.33.

71. Dunn, *The Partings of the Ways*, p. 31.

72. *Jos. Asen.* (trans. C. Burchard); in *OTP*, II, 8.5-7.

73. Barclay, *Jews in the Mediterranean Diaspora*, pp. 204-16.

recognized as a Torah requirement. According to Philo, Moses instructed the people: 'do not enter into the partnership of marriage with a member of a foreign nation, lest some day conquered by the forces of opposing customs you surrender and stray unawares from the path that leads to piety and turn aside into a pathless wild.'[74] Josephus noted Solomon's transgression of 'the laws of Moses who forbade marriage with persons of other races.'[75]

Paul's reminders to his readers of his pure heritage reflect the importance of endogamy within Judaism. He identified himself as an Israelite, a descendant of Abraham, a member of the tribe of Benjamin, and as a Hebrew of Hebrews (Rom. 11.1; 2 Cor. 11.22; Phil. 3.5). The willingness to distinguish between marriages where both partners were believers and marriages involving a believer and an unbeliever, granting greater freedom to divorce for those in 'mixed' marriages (1 Cor. 7.10-16), can be interpreted as a Pauline adaptation of Jewish endogamy.

The Jews' neighbors in the Greco-Roman world were aware of the Jewish practice of endogamy. Diodorus reproduced a comment that 'as to marriage and the burial of the dead, he [Moses] saw to it that their customs should differ widely from those of other men. But later, when they became subject to foreign rule, as a result of their mingling with men of other nations...many of their traditional practices were disturbed.'[76] Though Diodorus did not clarify how Jewish marriage practice differed, nor did he specify whether the practice of endogamy was 'disturbed', Tacitus's unflattering comments about Jewish sexuality suggest that endogamy endured as a distinctive and unadmired Jewish practice.[77]

Devotion to the Jerusalem Temple

For the hellenistic Diaspora, the Jerusalem temple and its cult have been described as 'the focal point of every aspect of Jewish national life', 'the centre of every aspect of national existence', 'the heart of Judaism', 'the vital support for the rest [of Judaism]', 'the center of Judaism', the 'unifying' symbol, and 'the magnetic field' drawing pilgrims 'from all points of the compass'.[78] Evidence supporting such

---

74. Philo, *Spec. Leg.* 3.29.
75. Josephus, *Ant* 8.191.
76. Diodorus Siculus, *Historical Library* 40.3.8.
77. Tacitus, *Histories* 5.5.
78. Wright, *The New Testament and the People of God*, pp. 224, 225, 226;

conclusions includes the practice of facing the Holy of Holies to pray at the times of the daily sacrifices and the throngs of pilgrims from the Diaspora that participated in the festival celebrations at the temple.[79] The magnitude of the temple's enduring symbolic power may be inferred from the persistence of temple sacrifices after the destruction of the sanctuary, the presence of menoroth as the 'most frequent by far' of the decorations in the Jewish catacomb inscriptions in Rome, the violent response to Hadrian's construction of a temple to Jupiter on the temple mount, and the plan of Emperor Julian to rebuild the temple almost three centuries after the destruction of 70 CE.[80]

Both Josephus and Philo demonstrated an interest in the temple. After praising his compatriots for their devotion to the Torah, Philo added that the Jewish people had even greater zeal for the temple (περιττοτέρα... ἡ περὶ τὸ ἱερὸν σπουδή, 'Still more abounding...is the zeal for the temple'), a passion whose depth was demonstrated by the execution of foreigners who entered the inner courts of the sanctuary.[81] Caligula's plan to erect his statue in the temple was described as a danger to 'not one part only of the Jewish race but the whole body of the nation'.[82] Josephus described the temple as the dwelling place of God, and he attributed the fall of Jerusalem and the destruction of the temple to the

Grabbe, *Judaism from Cyrus to Hadrian*, pp. 538, 540; *idem*, 'Hellenistic Judaism', p. 63; Barclay, *Jews in the Mediterranean Diaspora*, p. 419. Cf. Safrai, 'Relations between the Diaspora and the Land of Israel', pp. 186-87; A.T. Kraabel, 'Unity and Diversity among Diaspora Synagogues', in Lee I. Levine (ed.), *The Synagogue in Late Antiquity* (Philadelphia: The American Schools of Oriental Research, 1987), pp. 55-56.

79. Schürer, *The History of the Jewish People in the Age of Jesus Christ*, pp. 2:449, 454; Barclay, *Jews in the Mediterranean Diaspora*, p. 419; Graabe, *Judaism from Cyrus to Hadrian*, p. 538; *idem*, 'Hellenistic Judaism', p. 62; Safrai, 'Relations between the Diaspora and the Land of Israel', p. 186-87.

80. *m. Ed.* 8:6; Leon, *The Jews of Ancient Rome*, p. 196; Dio Cassius, *Roman History* 69.12.1; Julian, *Letter to the Community of the Jews*. Leon, discussing the specific symbolism of the menorah, concluded that the seven-branched candelabrum was a generic symbol of Judaism, detached from the temple cult, and functioning in a manner similar to the more modern *Magen David*; *The Jews of Ancient Rome*, pp. 197-98; 225-28. While Leon's conclusion may be valid for the later period treated in his study, clearly the source of the symbol was the temple menorah, and in the first century CE the menorah would have retained a symbolic association with the Jerusalem temple.

81. Philo, *Leg. Gai.* 212.

82. Philo, *Leg. Gai.* 184.

defiling of the sanctuary by assassins who shed blood in the temple courts.[83]

Grave concern for the sanctity of the temple was attributed to the Jewish people by the author of Luke–Acts. Both Stephen (Acts 6.13-14) and Paul (Acts 21.28; 24.6) were charged with threatening the sanctuary.

Greco-Roman authors were aware of the exclusive nature of the worship in the Jerusalem temple. Tacitus noted the exclusion of gentiles from the central precincts, and the exclusion of all but priests from the central sanctuary.[84] Diodorus preserved an account of the entrance of Antiochus Epiphanes into the Holy of Holies (εἰς τὸν ἄδυτον τοῦ θεοῦ σηκόν), a privilege granted by Jewish law only to 'the priest' (τὸν ἱερέα).[85] Plutarch's admission of ignorance regarding the manner of the celebration of Succot within the temple is probably a reflection of the exclusion of gentiles from that phase of the feast.[86]

Devotion to a temple and the exclusion of aliens from that sacred site contributed to the definition of the group, but one particular temple-related practice of diaspora Jews confirmed their distinctive existence within the larger Greco-Roman society. Cicero, defending a Roman official, stated:

> It was the practice each year to send gold to Jerusalem on the Jews' account from Italy and all our provinces, but Flaccus issued an edict forbidding its export from Asia. Who is there, gentlemen, who cannot genuinely applaud this measure? The Senate strictly forbade the export of gold on a considerable number of previous occasions, notably during my consulship. To oppose this outlandish superstition was an act of firmness, and to defy in the public interest the crowd of Jews that on occasion sets our public meetings ablaze was the height of responsibility... At Apamea a little less than a hundred pounds of gold was seized as it was being exported and weighed in the forum at the feet of the praetor through the efforts of Sextus Caesius, a thoroughly upright and honest Roman knight; at Laodicea a little more than twenty pounds was seized by Lucius Perducaeus who is here in court and a juror in this case; at Adramyttium a hundred pounds by Gnaeus Domitius, one of Flaccus' subordinate officers; at Pergamum not much... Every city, Laelius, has its own religious observances and we have ours. Even when Jerusalem was still standing and the Jews at peace with us, the demands of their

83. Josephus, *Ant.* 20.164-66.
84. Tacitus, *Histories* 5.8.
85. Diodorus Siculus, *Historical Library* 34/35.1.3.
86. Plutarch, *Quaestiones Conviviales* 4.6.2.

religion were incompatible with the majesty of our Empire, the dignity
of our name and the institutions of our ancestors; and now that the
Jewish nation has shown by armed rebellion what are its feelings for our
rule, they are even more so; how dear it was to the immortal gods has
been shown by the fact that it has been conquered [by Pompey, 63 BCE],
farmed out to the tax-collectors and enslaved.[87]

The temple tax, the source of the gold inventoried above, was a concrete means by which diaspora Jews could express their devotion to the
Jerusalem temple. Cicero's vehement reaction demonstrates that this
practice distinguished diaspora Jews from their neighbors. Similarly,
Tacitus complained that proselytes to Judaism 'always kept sending
tribute and contributions to Jerusalem, thereby increasing the wealth of
the Jews.'[88]

In defense of the temple tax, Josephus cited a decree by Augustus,
ordering that 'their sacred monies shall be inviolable and may be sent
up to Jerusalem and delivered to the treasurers in Jerusalem.'[89] Philo,
who was aware of the Augustan decree,[90] described the process
whereby every Jewish man 20 years and older participated cheerfully
and joyfully (φαιδροὶ καὶ γεγηθότες) in the financial support of the
temple.[91] The amount of confiscated gold detailed by Cicero suggests
that participation in the temple tax was widespread.

Resocialization of Proselytes

Converts to Judaism were seen as having realigned their social relationships and commitments.[92] Josephus distinguished between the status of
proselytes and the merely curious.

> To all who desire to come and live under the same laws as us, he
> [Moses] gives a gracious welcome, holding that it is not family ties alone
> which constitute relationship, but agreement in the principles of conduct.
> On the other hand, it was not his pleasure that casual visitors should be
> admitted to the intimacies of our daily life.[93]

87. Cicero, *Pro Flacco* 67-69.
88. Tacitus, *Histories* 5.5.
89. Josephus, *Ant.* 16.163.
90. Philo, *Leg. Gai.* 156, 291, 313.
91. Philo, *Spec. Leg.* 1.76-78.
92. Scot McKnight, *A Light among the Gentiles: Jewish Missionary Activity in
the Second Temple Period* (Minneapolis: Fortress Press, 1991), p. 47.
93. Josephus, *Apion* 2.210.

Philo was more explicit: proselytes 'have left...their country, their kinfolk and their friends for the sake of virtue and religion. Let them not be denied another citizenship or other ties of family and friendship, and let them find places of shelter standing ready for refugees to the camp of piety.'[94] Abraham was presented as the archetypal proselyte, having abandoned country, race, and family.[95]

An eschatological extension of the resocialization of proselytes is discernible in Paul's thought. With the arrival of the eschaton in Christ, the believer is a 'new creature/creation [κτίσις]' (2 Cor. 5.17).

Greco-Roman authors agreed that conversion to Judaism involved social reorientation, though they were less well disposed to the change. Seneca complained that 'the customs of this accursed race have gained such influence that they are now received throughout all the world. The vanquished have given laws to their victors.'[96] Juvenal mocked those who 'in time...take to circumcision. Having been wont to flout the laws of Rome, they learn and practise and revere the Jewish law.'[97] Tacitus was perhaps least reserved, denouncing 'the worst rascals among other peoples', who, after conversion, 'follow the same practice [i.e. circumcision], and the earliest lesson they receive is to despise the gods, to disown their country, and to regard their parents, children, and brothers as of little account.'[98] Dio Cassius reported that Tiberius's response to the large number of proselytes in Rome was to expel the Jews from the capital.[99]

Shaye Cohen introduced his study of conversion to Judaism in antiquity with the statement that 'in their minds and actions the Jews erected a boundary between themselves and the rest of humanity, the gentiles, but the boundary was always crossable and not always clearly marked.'[100] In his conclusions, Cohen described the 'boundary that separates Jews and Judaism from pagans and paganism' as 'distinct but broad'.[101] Traversing that boundary required practice of the Torah,

94. Philo, *Spec. Leg.* 1.52. Cf. *idem, Virt.* 102-103, 108.
95. Philo, *Virt.* 212-19.
96. Seneca quoted in Augustine, *The City of God* 6.11.
97. Juvenal, *Satires* 14.99-101.
98. Tacitus, *Histories* 5.5.
99. Dio Cassius, *Roman History* 57.18.5a.
100. Shaye J. D. Cohen, 'Crossing the Boundary and Becoming a Jew', *HTR* 82 (1989), pp. 13-33 (13).
101. Cohen, 'Crossing the Boundary', p. 31.

aniconic monotheism, and the resocialization of the proselyte.[102]

Based on *m. Ker.* 2.1, S. Safrai concluded that conversion was incomplete until the proselyte had offered a sacrifice in the temple.[103] The mishnah noted by Safrai is attributed to a rabbi who was active in the period immediately after the fall of Jerusalem (80–110 CE), and the requirement for proselytes to offer a sacrifice would be an unlikely addition after the destruction of the temple, so this halakah can be presumed reasonably to have been in effect before 70 CE. Such a cultic act on the part of the proselyte would have served to reinforce the new identification with the Jewish people.

Unity of Judea and the Diaspora

Explicit statements of unity between diaspora Jews and those of the homeland are lacking in the writings of Greco-Roman authors. Insinuations of such a connection are evident, however. In his epistle to the people of Alexandria, Claudius responded to the riots in that city with a variety of warnings, including an order to the Jewish residents of Alexandria 'not to bring in or admit Jews who come down the river from Syria or Egypt, a proceeding which will compel me to conceive serious suspicions.'[104] The implied willingness of non-Alexandrian Jews to enter into the conflict on the side of their co-religionists suggests that a social bond existed between geographically separated Jewish communities, and that bond was stronger than the social links among the various residents of Alexandria. A comparable conclusion may be drawn from the imposition of the *Fiscus Iudaicus* in the aftermath of the Jewish revolt of 66–73 CE. Though the rebellion was limited to the Jewish homeland, Suetonius referred to the tax as being levied on all the Jewish people, including those residing in the Diaspora.[105] This act implies that, though the diaspora Jews were non-participants in the rebellion, the stigma of the revolt was associated with the entire Jewish nation, of which the diaspora Jews were an integral component.[106]

In the writings of Philo and Josephus all Jews are viewed as a single people. Recognizing the physical distance separating Jewish communi-

102. Cohen, 'Crossing the Boundary', p. 26.
103. Safrai, 'Relations between the Diaspora and the Land of Israel', p. 187.
104. Claudius, *Letter of Claudius to the Alexandrians* 96-98.
105. Suetonius, *Domitian* 12.2.
106. Cf. Barclay, *Jews in the Mediterranean Diaspora*, p. 407.

ties, Josephus reported that one of the purposes of the pilgrim festivals was to ensure that the people 'should not be ignorant of one another, being members of the same race and partners in the same institutions.'[107] Though his explicit reference was to 'the ends of the land which the Hebrews shall conquer',[108] Josephus's statement is relevant to the Jewish Diaspora. As a life-long resident of the Diaspora, Philo commented more frequently on the relationship between Diaspora and homeland, finding the same function in the festivals.

> Countless multitudes from countless cities come, some over land, others over sea, from east and west and north and south at every feast... Friendships are formed between those who hitherto knew not each other, and the sacrifices and libations are the occasion of reciprocity of feeling and constitute the surest pledge that all are of one mind.[109]

Thus unified, the Jewish people constituted a single nation, unlimited in number, residing in almost the whole habitable world, ready to come to the common defense.[110]

In Acts, the Jewish people are presented as a unified group. The descriptions of diaspora participation in the feasts (Acts 2.5-11) and the temple cultus (Acts 21.27) are in harmony with the assertions of Philo and Josephus. The apparent residence of diaspora Jews in Jerusalem (Acts 6.9) and the self-identification of Jews in Rome with other Jews (Acts 28.17, 21) reinforce the conclusion that a significant degree of unity existed between Judean and diaspora Jews.

Assessing the Group Status of First-Century CE Hellenistic Judaism

The strong group status of first-century CE hellenistic Judaism is evident in the multifaceted, interwoven expressions of group identity. Six elements of Jewish identity have been noted and the significance of each element in distinguishing Jews from gentiles has been discussed. The ubiquity of recognition of these group defining characteristics is suggested by the references noted in table 3.[111]

---

107. Josephus, *Ant.* 4.204.
108. Josephus, *Ant.* 4.203.
109. Philo, *Spec. Leg.* 1.69-70.
110. Philo, *Leg. Gai.* 214-15. Cf. *idem*, *Leg. Gai.* 194, 281-82.
111. Not all of the references identified in table 3 are cited in the above discussion.

Table 3. References to Jewish boundary markers by Greco-Roman authors

Author	Aniconic Monotheism	Torah as a Central Symbol	Practice of the Torah*	Devotion to the Jerusalem Temple	Resocializaton of Proselytes	Unity of Judea and the Diaspora
Diodorus	HL 40.3.4	HL 1.94.1-2; 34/35.1.4; 40.3.3	HL 1.28.2-3 [c] HL 34/35.1.2,4 [d] HL 40.3.8 [e]	HL 34/35.1.3-4 HL 40.3.4		
Cicero				Pro Flacco 66-69		
Strabo	Geog 16.2.35		Geog 16.2.37, 40 [a, c, d]			
Claudius						Letter to the Alexandrians
Seneca		Augustine City 6.11	Augustine City 6.11 [a] Epist. 95.47-48 [a]		Augustine City 6.11	
Petronius			Satyricon 102.14 [c]			
Plutarch			Q. C. 4.5.1-3 [d] Q. C. 4.6.2 [a, b]	Q. C. 4.6.2		
Tacitus	Hist. 5.5, 9	Hist. 5.4	Hist. 5.4-5 [a, b, c, d, e]	Hist. 5.5, 8	Hist. 5.5	
Suetonius			Domitian 12.2 [c]			Domitian 12.2
Juvenal	Sat. 14.97	Sat. 6.544; 14.100-101	Sat. 14.96-99 [a, c, d]		Sat. 14.99-101	
Dio Cassius	RH 37.17.2; 67.14.2, 69.12.1-2		RH 37.16.2; 37.17.3; 49.22.4-5 [a]	RH 37.17.3; 49.22.4-5; 69.12.1-2	RH 38.17.1; 57.18.5a	
Philostratus	Life 5.33		Life 5.33 [d]			

* Practice of the Torah: a. Sabbath Observance; b. Feasts and Fasts; c. Circumcision; d. Kashrut and Table Fellowship; e. Endogamy

Two comments cited above require elaboration. Grabbe stated that 'the one area where Jews did find themselves at odds with the rest of the Hellenistic world was in the area of religion. They alone of all ethnic groups refused to honor gods, shrines and cults other than their own.'[112] His intent was not to argue that aniconic monotheism was the only boundary marker between Jews and gentiles; elsewhere he identified circumcision, kashrut, the centrality of the Torah, Sabbath, and devotion to the Jerusalem temple as essential components of Jewish life.[113] Rather, Grabbe was stressing the fact that although the Jews accepted the practices of others (e.g. they did not seek to impose sabbath regulations on gentiles), this open-minded attitude did not extend to worship; Jews denied the legitimacy of all foreign gods and cults.

Cohen's description of the boundary separating Jews from gentiles as 'always crossable and not always clearly marked' was not intended to suggest that Jews were poorly differentiated from gentiles.[114] Stating his conclusions, Cohen described 'the boundary that separates Jews and Judaism from pagans and paganism' as 'distinct but broad'.[115] The ambiguity to which he referred was limited to the status of gentiles who identified themselves with Judaism. Cohen identified seven categories of affiliation, ranging from 'admiring some aspect of Judaism' to 'converting to Judaism and "becoming a Jew".'[116] Individuals falling into any of these categories could be viewed as 'crossing the boundary', but their status was nebulous, even if they were recognized as proselytes.[117]

The sketch of first-century CE hellenistic Judaism presented above differs little from the Judaism of the homeland. E.P. Sanders listed the symbolic significance of the Torah, devotion to the Jerusalem temple, observance of holy days, sabbath observance, circumcision, and monotheism as aspects of Common Judaism.[118] Sanders acknowledged the correlation between the Judaism of Judea and the Judaism of the Mediterranean Diaspora.[119]

---

112. Grabbe, 'Hellenistic Judaism', p. 73.
113. Grabbe, 'Hellenistic Judaism', p. 71; *idem, Judaism from Cyrus to Hadrian*, pp. 528-29, 538-40, 542.
114. Cohen, 'Crossing the Boundary', p. 13.
115. Cohen, 'Crossing the Boundary', p. 31.
116. Cohen, 'Crossing the Boundary', pp. 15-30.
117. Cohen, 'Crossing the Boundary', p. 29.
118. Sanders, *Judaism: Practice and Belief*, pp. 47-48, 236-37, 242.
119. Sanders, *Judaism: Practice and Belief*, p. 47.

Two factors contributed to this harmony within first-century CE Judaism. First was the unity of Judea and the Diaspora, discussed above. Second was the fact that Judean Judaism was itself hellenized. Martin Hengel concluded that

> from about the middle of the third century BC all *Judaism* must really be designated '*Hellenistic Judaism*' in the strict sense... These circumstances make the differentiation between 'Palestinian' and 'Hellenistic' Judaism, which is one of the fundamental heuristic principles of New Testament scholarship, much more difficult; indeed, on the whole it proves to be no longer adequate' (emphasis original).[120]

Grabbe summarized the principal differences between the Jews of Israel and those of the Diaspora as: (1) geographical separation from the temple and (2) the experience of living as a minority community in a largely pagan setting,[121] both of which could be applied to a lesser extent to the Jews of Galilee.

One caution should be noted relative to the sketch of Judaism presented above. A description of the boundaries of Jewish identity must not be confused for an account of the experience of living as a Jew. Neusner criticized Sanders's portrait of 'common denominator-Judaism' because of the lack of individualism, local nuance, internal conflict, and vivid passion.[122] The same criticism would apply to the above presentation if the skeletal group boundary was mistaken for the living society.

Grid Characteristics of Hellenistic Judaism

Temple and Torah as Grid Markers

With Douglas's equation of strong grid with 'visible rules about space and time related to social roles',[123] devotion to the Jerusalem temple and practice of the Torah must be recognized as major components of the grid strength of first-century CE hellenistic Judaism. The temple was the symbolic heart of pre-70 CE Judaism, and the explicit limitations on

---

120. Martin Hengel, *Judaism and Hellenism: Studies in their Encounter in Palestine during the Early Hellenistic Period*, I (2 vols.; trans. John Bowden; Philadelphia: Fortress Press, 1974), pp. 104-105.

121. Grabbe, *Judaism From Cyrus to Hadrian*, p. 531.

122. Jacob Neusner, review of *Judaism: Practice and Belief 63 BCE67 CE* (London: SCM Press; Philadelphia: Trinity Press International, 1992), by E.P. Sanders, in *JSJ* 24 (1993), pp. 318-19, 322.

123. Douglas, 'Cultural Bias', p. 192.

access constituted spatial regulation. As stated above, both Tacitus and Diodorus noted the exclusion of all but priests from the holiest precincts and Tacitus mentioned the prohibition of gentiles from the temple. While the latter regulation, against gentiles, is relevant for an assessment of group strength, the privileged access granted to priests serves as an indicator of grid strength.

Josephus provided the following description of the temple:

> Within it [the first court] and not far distant was a second one, accessible by a few steps and surrounded by a stone balustrade with an inscription prohibiting the entrance of a foreigner under threat of the penalty of death. On its southern and northern sides the inner court had three-chambered gateways, equally distant from one another, and on the side where the sun rises it had one great gateway, through which those of us who were ritually clean used to pass with our wives. Within this court was the sacred (court) which women were forbidden to enter, and still farther within was a third court into which only priests were permitted to go. In this (priests' court) was the temple, and before it was an altar on which we used to sacrifice whole burnt-offerings to God.[124]

This account provides evidence for 'visible rules about space…related to social roles', the social roles being reflected in distinctions between men and women and between the priesthood and the laity. Enhancing the grid significance of these rules is the asymmetry and entitlement of the roles; levitical priesthood and male gender are not exchangeable with their counterparts and are consequences of birth, not achievement.

A third grid predicate, accountability, is evident in the threat of execution inscribed on the stone balustrade separating gentiles from Jews.[125] Paul's arrest, based on the charge that, by bringing gentiles into

---

124. Josephus, *Ant.* 15.417-19; cf. *idem*, *War* 5.193-200.

125. A photograph of one of these inscriptions, with a transcription and translation, is presented in Adolf Deissmann, *Light from the Ancient East: The New Testament Illustrated by Recently Discovered Texts of the Graeco-Roman World* (trans. Lionel R.M. Strachan; New York: George H. Doran Company, 4th edn, 1927), pp. 80-81, and a transcription is presented in Schürer, *The History of the Jewish People*, II, p. 285. Schürer's transcription and Diesmann's translation follow:

ΜΗΘΕΝΑ ΑΛΛΟΓΕΝΗ ΕΙΣΠΟ	Let no foreigner enter
ΡΕΥΕΣΘΑΙ ΕΝΤΟΣ ΤΟΥ ΠΕ	within the screen and
ΡΙ ΤΟ ΙΕΡΟΝ ΤΡΥΦΑΚΤΟΥ ΚΑΙ	enclosure surrounding the
ΠΕΡΙΒΟΛΟΥ ΟΣ Δ ΑΝ ΛΗ	sanctuary. Whoever is taken
ΦΘΗ ΕΑΥΤΩΙ ΑΙΤΙΟΣ ΕΣ	in so doing will be the

the temple, 'he has defiled this holy place' (Acts 21.28), is an example of the force of this prohibition and of the strength of feeling against those thought to have violated the sanctuary.

Complementing the spatial regulation, made concrete in the architecture of the temple, were the temporal regulations of the Torah regarding the sabbath and the feasts and fasts. While the group-defining character of these aspects of Torah praxis was discussed above, celebration of these holy days served also to reinforce the grid of social roles in first-century CE hellenistic Judaism.

Festal pilgrimage placed the worshipper in the temple, the grid implications of which have been identified. In the Diaspora frequent participation in the festal pilgrimages would have been the privilege of the wealthier members of the community, thus highlighting the status of the pilgrim. For those who resided in the Diaspora during the feasts, celebration included a communal meal.[126] Such banquets function sociologically to confirm the hierarchy and social stratification of the feasting community, reflected in a 'concern over the seating arrangement of those eating, a ranking in terms of some value or honor system.'[127] The grid implications of a community meal lay at the heart of Jesus' parable in Lk. 14.7-11 and in Jesus' censure in Lk. 20.46. An example of a 'value or honor system' that influenced the status of participants at the feast is the patron-client relationship. By providing the food and/or facilities for a community banquet, an individual could establish or maintain a position of honor among the feasting group,[127] thus reinforcing the grid of the society.

TAI ΔIA TO EΞAKOΛOΥ   cause that death
ΘEIN ΘANATON   overtaketh him.

Cf. Philo, *Leg. Gai.* 212.

126. Schürer, *The History of the Jewish People*, III, pp. 144-45; citing Josephus, *Ant.* 14.216; Philo, *Vit. Mos.* 2.42; Plutarch, *Quaestiones Conviviales* 4.6.2.

127. Jerome H. Neyrey, 'Ceremonies in Luke–Acts: The Case of Meals and Table Fellowship', in Jerome H. Neyrey (ed.), *The Social World of Luke Acts: Models for Interpretation* (Peabody, MA: Hendrickson, 1991), pp. 361-87 (366); cf. Mary Douglas, 'Deciphering a Meal', *Daedalus* 101 (1972), pp. 61-81 (61); Malina and Rohrbaugh, *Social-Science Commentary on the Synoptic Gospels*, pp. 366-68; Jerome H. Neyrey, 'Meals, Food, and Table Fellowship', in Richard L. Rohrbaugh (ed.), *The Social Sciences and New Testament Interpretation* (Peabody, MA: Hendrickson, 1996), pp. 159-82 (171).

128. Halvor Moxnes, 'Patron-Client Relations and the New Community in Luke-Acts', in Jerome H. Neyrey (ed.), *The Social World of Luke Acts: Models for Inter-*

Synagogue worship on the sabbath and in conjunction with the feasts and fasts was more egalitarian than the temple cult.

> The people were deeply attached to the worship offered in the Temple, but that such worship could be offered at all depended on the presence of the priests. In the synagogue, on the other hand, divine service depended on the congregation, and not on the priests... Indeed, the whole institution was based on public participation, and it was this communal character which gave it its special status.[129]

Direct lay involvement in synagogue worship should not, however, be confused for a lack of hierarchy in the synagogue.

As was the case at communal meals, seating in the synagogue reflected the status of the individual. The author of Luke–Acts quoted Jesus' denunciation of those who sought the best seats (πρωτοκαθεδρία; Lk. 11.43; 20.46) in the synagogue. Further distinction in the synagogue existed in the presumed segregation of men and women.[130]

Though the synagogue was not a priestly institution, priests received certain privileges in the synagogue. Pronouncing the priestly benediction was a priestly prerogative[131] and priests were given preference in the selection of an individual to read from and expound on the scriptures.[132]

Extant inscriptions and texts preserve several titles associated with

pretation (Peabody, MA: Hendrickson, 1991), pp. 241-68 (249); Neyrey, 'Ceremonies in Luke–Acts', pp. 373-74; Bruce J. Malina, *The New Testament World: Insights from Cultural Anthropology* (Louisville: Westminster/John Knox Press, 2nd edn, 1993), pp. 100-102; John Hall Elliott, 'Patronage and Clientage', in Richard L. Rohrbaugh (ed.), *The Social Sciences and New Testament Interpretation* (Peabody, MA: Hendrickson, 1996), pp. 144-52 (149).

129. S. Safrai, 'The Synagogue', in. S. Safrai, M. Stern, D. Flusser, and W.C. van Unnik (eds.) *The Jewish People in the First Century: Historical Geography, Political History, Social, Cultural and Religious Life and Institutions* (CRINT; Assen: Van Gorcum, 1974), pp. 908-44 (915); cf. Lee I. Levine, 'The Second Temple Synagogue: The Formative Years', in Lee I. Levine (ed.) *The Synagogue in Late Antiquity* (Philadelphia: The American Schools of Oriental Research, 1987), pp. 7-31 (7); Kraabel, 'Unity and Diversity among Diaspora Synagogues', p. 54.

130. Schürer, *The History of the Jewish People*, II, p. 447. Though no literary source states that men and women were separated from one another in the synagogue, the practice in the temple and the evidence of the architecture of ancient Galilean synagogues supports the presumption that segregation was practiced.

131. *m. Meg.* 4:3; cf. Schürer, *The History of the Jewish People*, II, p. 448.

132. Philo, *Hypothetica*, cited in Eusebius, *Preparation for the Gospel* 360a.

the synagogue and/or the Jewish community: ἀρχισυνάγωγος, 'synagogue ruler', ἄρχων, 'ruler', γερουσιάρχης, 'council ruler', ἀρχιγερουσιάρχης, 'ruler of council rulers', πρεσβύτερος, 'elder', γραμματεύς, 'secretary', ψαλμῳδός, 'cantor', ὑπηρέτης, 'attendant', διάκονος, 'servant', *pater synagogae*, 'father of the synagogue', and *mater synagogae* 'mother of the synagogue'. The precise roles or functions of the individuals to whom these titles were granted are not clear, and may have varied from one location to another (e.g. the more centralized authority of the community of Alexandria versus the apparently decentralized community of Rome).[133] Resolution of the details of community organization is, however, unnecessary for the present study. A consensus exists that at least some of these titles were associated closely with the synagogue and that at least some of them recognized the honored status of the individual (whether or not an actual function was associated with the title); therefore, participation in the life of the synagogue involved participation in a society that bestowed honor on and/or entrusted power to selected individuals. Stated in terms of Douglas's paradigm, participation in the life of the synagogue involved participation in a society with at least some strong grid characteristics.

Based on an equation of the ὑπηρέτης/διάκονος, 'attendant/servant', with the חזן הכנסת, 'minister', and on the mishnaic prescriptions in *m. Mak.* 3.12, Schürer concluded that the ὑπηρέτης/διάκονος was responsible for carrying out corporal punishment on those sentenced to scourging by the synagogue/community.[134] Confirmation of the practice of synagogue-based corporal punishment in the first century CE exists in the testimony of Paul as the dispenser (Acts 26.11) and as the recipient (2 Cor. 11.24) of communal discipline. Such accountability is characteristic of strong grid societies.[135]

---

133. Schürer, *The History of the Jewish People*, II, pp. 427-39; III, pp. 87-107; Leon, *The Jews of Ancient Rome*, pp. xvii, 167-94.

134. Schürer, *The History of the Jewish People*, II, p. 438.

135. Gross and Rayner, *Measuring Culture*, pp. 81-82.

Social Stratification in Hellenistic Judaism

> Ten castes came up from Babylonia: priests, Levites, Israelites, impaired priests, converts, and freed slaves, *mamzers*, *Netins*, 'silenced ones' [*shetuqi*], and foundlings. Priests, Levites, and Israelites are permitted to marry among one another. Levites, Israelites, impaired priests, converts, and freed slaves are permitted to marry among one another. Converts, freed slaves, *mamzers*, *Netins*, 'silenced ones', and foundlings are permitted to marry among one another.
>
> And what are 'silenced ones'? Any who knows the identity of his mother but does not know the identity of his father. And foundlings? Any who was discovered in the market and knows neither his father nor his mother. Abba Saul did call a 'silenced one' [*shetuqi*] 'one who is to be examined' [*beduqi*].
>
> All those who are forbidden from entering into the congregation are permitted to marry one another. R. Judah prohibits. R. Eliezer says, 'Those who are of certain status are permitted to intermarry with others who are of certain status. Those who are of certain status and those who are of doubtful status, those who are of doubtful status and those who of certain status, those who are of doubtful status and those who are of doubtful status—it is prohibited.' And who are those who are of doubtful status? The 'silenced one', the foundling, and the Samaritan.[136]

This mishnah describes a complex, stratified society. Distinct groups, as defined here, are identified in table 4. If this scheme could be dated to the first century CE, the identification of first-century Judaism as a strong grid society would be assured. Tal Ilan stated that 'the indication that these stocks "came up from Babylonia" appears to be historically authentic.'[137] Conversely, Neusner concluded that 'there seems to me no reason to doubt that the whole derives from the second century.'[138] Because of this discrepancy, the correlation between the mishnaic description of Jewish society and the actual conditions in the first-century CE must be determined.

---

136. *m. Qid.* 4.1-3; all quotations from the Mishnah are taken from *The Mishnah: A New Translation* (trans. Jacob Neusner, New Haven: Yale University Press, 1988).

137. Tal Ilan, *Jewish Women in Greco-Roman Palestine* (Peabody, MA: Hendrickson, 1995), p. 70.

138. Jacob Neusner, *A History of the Mishnaic Law of Women*. V. *The Mishnaic System of Women* (SJLA; Leiden: E.J. Brill, 1980), p. 175.

Table 4. *Stratification of Jewish society according to* m. Qid. *4.1-3*

Priests	Group I permitted to marry Group I or II
Levites Israelites	Group II permitted to marry Group I, II, III or IV
Impaired Priests	Group III permitted to marry Group II, III or IV
Converts Freed Slaves	Group IV permitted to marry Group II, III, IV, V or VI (?)*
Mamzers *Netins*	Group V permitted to marry Group IV, V or VI (?)*
Shetuqi Foundlings	Group VI permitted (?)* to marry Group IV, V or VI
Those excluded from the synagogue Samaritans	Marginal groups permitted to marry each other (?)*

*   Marriageability of Group VI and of Samaritans was denied by *R. Eliezer*,
and marriageability of those excluded from the synagogue was denied by
R. Judah. Presumably marginal groups would have been relatively uncon-
cerned about rabbinical regulation of marriage.

Priesthood. Declarations of the high status of priests are abundant in
first-century CE literature. Proclaiming his own honorable status, Josephus opened his autobiography by stating: 'My family is no ignoble
one, tracing its descent far back to priestly ancestors. Different races
base their claim to nobility on various grounds; with us a connexion
with the priesthood is the hallmark of an illustrious line.'[139]

Marriage regulations reflect the aristocratic status of the priesthood.
Philo stated that a priest must marry 'a pure virgin whose parents and
grandparents and ancestors are equally pure, highly distinguished for

139. Josephus, *Life* 1.

the excellence of their conduct and lineage.'[140] This requirement would have the effect of prohibiting the marriage of a priest to a proselyte or to the daughter of a proselyte. More strict was the regulation of the marriage of the high priest: 'The high priest must not propose marriage save to one who is not only a virgin but a priestess descended from priests.'[141] Josephus noted that a priest was not permitted to marry a slave or a captive and that a blemished priest was denied access to the altar and to the Holy Place.[142] Confirming Philo's statement that the prospective wife of a priest must have a distinguished lineage, Josephus reported that, prior to marriage,

> he must investigate her pedigree, obtaining the genealogy from the archives and producing a number of witnesses. And this practice of ours is not confined to the home country of Judaea, but wherever there is a Jewish colony, there too a strict account is kept by the priests of their marriages; I allude to the Jews in Egypt and Babylon and other parts of the world in which any of the priestly order are living in dispersion. A statement is drawn up by them and sent to Jerusalem, showing the names of the bride and her father and more remote ancestors, together with the names of the witnesses.[143]

Josephus affirmed that his own priestly lineage could be confirmed in the public register.[144]

The elevated status of the priesthood is reflected in other contemporary texts. Diodorus stated that the ruler of the Jews was 'called High Priest, not King', and that 'the Jews never have a king, and authority over the people is regularly vested in whichever priest is regarded as superior to his colleagues in wisdom and virtue. They call this man the high priest, and believe that he acts as a messenger to them of God's commandments.'[145] In his description of the ruling council before which Peter and John appeared, the author of Luke–Acts mentioned specifically 'Annas the high priest and Caiaphas and John and Alexander and whoever was of the high-priestly family' (Acts 4.6). Later in

---

140. Philo *Spec. Leg.* 1.101.
141. Philo *Spec. Leg.* 1.110.
142. Josephus, *Ant.* 3.276-78.
143. Josephus, *Apion* 1.31-33.
144. Josephus, *Life* 6.
145. Diodorus Siculus, *Historical Library* 40.2.1, 40.3.5. In a later century, Dio Cassius equated the priesthood and the kingdom: ἱερωσύνης (οὕτω γὰρ τὴν βασιλείαν σφῶν ὠνόμαζον), *Roman History* 37.15.2.

the same document, Paul, though a prisoner, is quoted as acknowledging the dignity of the high-priesthood (Acts 23.1-5). The desirability of
a priest marrying the daughter of a priest is suggested in the description
of the pious parents of John the Baptist (Lk. 1.5-6).[146]

These data support the conclusion that the priesthood constituted a
nobility characterized by asymmetry and entitlement, indicative of a
strong grid society. This interpretation is consistent with Grabbe's
statement that 'the civil institutions below emperor and king were
dominated by the priesthood, especially the "chief priests' and M.
Stern's description of the high-priestly families as an oligarchy.[147]

Levites. References to the Levites as a class distinct from the priests are
fewer than references to the priests themselves. In his description of the
celebration of Succot, Plutarch mentioned the participants who
'advance playing harps; these players are called in their language
Levites'.[148] This comment suggests that the Levites had a cultic role
separate from the altar and the Holy Place/Holy of Holies. More
explicit was Philo's account:

> After bestowing these great sources of revenue on the priests, he did not
> ignore those of the second rank, namely the temple attendants. Some of
> these are stationed at the doors as gatekeepers at the very entrances,
> some within in front of the sanctuary to prevent any unlawful person
> from setting foot thereon, either intentionally or unintentionally. Some
> patrol around it turn by turn in relays by appointment night and day,
> keeping watch and guard at both seasons. Others sweep the porticoes and
> the open court, convey away the refuse and ensure cleanliness.[149]

With this description of the role of the Levites, the assigned status of
the Levites can be determined as intermediate between the priesthood
and the laity.

Proselytes. Conversion as resocialization to a new group was discussed
above; the issue to be addressed here is the status of the proselyte in the

146. Cf. Bock, *Luke 1:1–9:50*, pp. 76-77.
147. Grabbe, *Judaism from Cyrus to Hadrian*, II, p. 545; M. Stern, 'Aspects of
Jewish Society: The Priesthood and Other Classes', in. S. Safrai, M. Stern, D.
Flusser and W.C. van Unnik (eds.), *The Jewish People in the First Century: Historical Geography, Political History, Social, Cultural and Religious Life and Institutions* (CRINT; Assen: Van Gorcum, 1976), p. 603.
148. Plutarch, *Quaestiones Conviviales* 4.6.2.
149. Philo, *Spec. Leg.* 1.156.

new group. Ideally, the proselyte was welcomed as a full member of the nation. Referring to 'our legislator', Josephus stated that 'to all who desire to come and live under the same laws with us, he gives a gracious welcome.'[150] Philo elaborated:

> All of like sort to him [Moses], all who spurn idle fables and embrace truth in its purity, whether they have been such from the first or through conversion to the better side have reached that higher state, obtain His approval, the former because they were not false to the nobility of their birth, the latter because their judgement led them to make the passage to piety. These last he calls 'proselytes [προσηλύτους],' or newly-joined, because they have joined the new and godly commonwealth. Thus, while giving equal rank to all in-comers [ἐπηλύτας] with all the privileges which he gives to the native-born, he exhorts the old nobility to honour them not only with marks of respect but with special friendship and with more than ordinary goodwill.
>
> Having laid down laws for members of the same nation, he holds that the incomers [ἐπηλύτας] too should be accorded every favour and consideration as their due... He commands all members of the nation to love the incomers, not only as friends and kinsfolk but as themselves both in body and soul: in bodily matters, by acting as far as may be for their common interest; in mental by having the same griefs and joys, so that they might seem to be the separate parts of a single living being which is compacted and unified by their fellowship in it.[151]

These declarations place the proselyte on the same stratum as the native-born Israelite. The question remains, however, are these assertions descriptive or prescriptive?

After continuing the above discourse with a discussion of the treatment of foreigners seeking exile [μέτοικος] among the Jews, Philo added:

> And if any of them [i.e. the new-comers, τοῖς ἥκουσι] should wish to pass over into the Jewish community, they must not be spurned with an unconditional refusal as children of enemies, but be so far favoured that the third generation is invited to the congregation and made partakers in the divine revelations, to which also the native born, whose lineage is beyond reproach, are rightfully admitted.[152]

This comment is consistent with the inference drawn above, that neither a proselyte nor the daughter of a proselyte could marry a priest, leaving

---

150. Josephus, *Apion* 2.210.
151. Philo, *Spec. Leg.* 1.51-52; *idem, Virt.* 102-103.
152. Philo, *Virt.* 108.

open the possibility that in the third generation such a marriage could be considered.

Another hint regarding the status of proselytes has an origin in the practice of the translators of the Septuagint. All occurrences of προσήλυτος in the Septuagint are translations of גר, frequently in the formula, 'strangers, orphans, and widows' (Deut. 10.18; 14.29; 16.11, 14; 24.17, 19 [adding 'the poor'], 20, 21; 26.12, 13; 27.19).[153] Employing this formula, Philo described God's concern for the lowly: 'Yet vast as are his [God's] excellences and powers, he takes pity and compassion on those most helplessly in need, and does not disdain to give judgement to strangers [προσηλύτοις] or orphans or widows. He holds their low estate worthy of His providential care, while of kings and despots and great potentates He takes no account.'[154] Because of this formula, Jews who were more familiar with the Septuagint than with the Hebrew text (i.e. Hellenistic Jews) would have found grounds for associating proselytes with the lowly, weak members of society.[155]

A further comment suggests that proselytes were the object of some disdain. Philo described the mixed multitude that accompanied the children of Israel in the exodus from Egypt as 'a promiscuous, nondescript and menial crowd, a bastard-host, so to speak, associated with the true-born.' In addition to the offspring of Israelite fathers and Egyptian mothers, this population included 'those who, reverencing the divine favour shewn to the people, had come over to them, and such as were converted [ἐπηλύται ἐγένοντο] and brought to a wiser mind by the magnitude and the number of the successive punishments.'[156]

Based on the third-generation requirement for full acceptance, the potential for associating proselytes with the weakest members of society, and the association of proselytes with 'a promiscuous, nondescript and menial crowd, a bastard-host', the requirement that proselytes be

153. J. Lust, E. Eynikel and K. Hauspie, *A Greek-English Lexicon of the Septuagint*. II. *K–W* (Stuttgart: Deutsche Bibelgesellschaft, 1996), p. 402.

154. Philo, *Spec. Leg.* 1.308.

155. In four of the references noted above (Deut. 14.29; 16.11, 14; 26.12, 13) Levites are included in the formula. Levites were not, however, placed on the same level as the stranger, orphan, and widow. The inclusion of the Levites is explained in Deut. 14.29: 'for he has neither share nor portion with you,' a phrase not applied to the stranger, orphan, or widow (translation from the Septuagint by the author, based on *Septuaginta: Id est Vetus Testamentum graece iuxta LXX interpretes*, ed. Alfred Rahlfs [Stuttgart: Deutsche Bibelgesellschaft, 1935, 1979]).

156. Philo, *Vit. Mos.* 1.147.

granted a status equal to that of a native-born Israelite should be recognized as prescription rather than description. Martin Goodman's reference to 'the ambiguous status of proselytes in the eyes of Jews' is an apt characterization.[157] Noting the common practice in epitaphs and synagogue inscriptions of attaching the label 'proselyte' to the name of a convert, Cohen reached the same conclusion as Goodman: 'the proselyte probably had an ambiguous status in the Jewish community.'[158] Corroborating evidence for the conclusion that proselytes were usually identified as such within Jewish society is the description of the Pentecost pilgrims in Acts: 'both Jews and proselytes' (Acts 2.11).

Captives and Slaves. In the discussion of the priesthood, Josephus's record of the prohibition of marriage between a priest and a slave or a prisoner of war was noted. Based on 'decorum and the proprieties of rank' Josephus transmitted a further prohibition against any free man marrying a slave, 'however strongly some may be constrained thereto by love [ἔρως].'[159] Josephus's comments reflect the fact that, in addition to working as a household servant, a female slave was expected to provide sexual gratification for the males of the household and was, therefore, an unsuitable bride.[160] While Josephus did not mention explicitly female prisoners of war in the regulation of marriage for all free Israelites, the sexual exploitation of female captives would have raised similar questions about their suitability for marriage.[161]

Marginal Groups. Prostitutes were members of a stratum distinct from that occupied by Israelites of good reputation. Discussing the laws regulating the marriage of priests, Philo explained that:

> a harlot is profane in body and soul, even if she had discarded her trade and assumed a decent and chaste demeanour, and he [the priest] is forbidden even to approach her, since her old way of living was unholy. Let

---

157. Martin Goodman, *Mission and Conversion: Proselytizing in the Religious History of the Roman Empire* (Oxford: Clarendon Press, 1994), p. 85. Cf. McKnight, *A Light among the Gentiles*, pp. 30-48; Louis H. Feldman, *Jew and Gentile in the Ancient World: Attitudes and Interactions from Alexander to Justinian* (Princeton: Princeton University Press, 1993), pp. 338-41.

158. Cohen, 'Crossing the Boundary', p. 29.

159. Josephus, *Ant.* 4.244.

160. Ilan, *Jewish Women*, p. 206.

161. Ilan, *Jewish Women*, pp. 220-21.

such a one indeed retain in other respects her civic rights as she has been
at pains to purge herself from her defilements, for repentance from
wrongdoing is praiseworthy. Nor let anyone else be prevented from taking her in marriage, but let her not come near to the priest.[162]

Josephus concurred in the case of the priest and extended the prohibition to the marriage of a harlot with any Israelite.[163] The reason stated
for the extension, that God would not accept her nuptial sacrifices, may
have applied only to an unrepentant, practicing prostitute.[164]

In the Lucan account of the anointing of Jesus, the woman who
approached Jesus is introduced by the narrator as 'a sinner', and the
host, a Pharisee, concurred (Lk. 7.37, 39). The specific 'sin' of which
this woman was guilty was probably prostitution, an occupation render-
ing her unsuitable for marriage with an honorable Israelite and earning
for her the designation 'sinner'. As presented in Luke, a 'sinner' was
one to whom an honorable person would deny table fellowship (Lk.
5.30; 15.2; 19.7), and would probably have qualified as one 'forbidden
from entering into the congregation'.[165]

Based on the common association of 'sinners and tax collectors' (Lk.
5.30; 7.34; 15.1), prostitutes and tax collectors would have been
classified together as people who, though they were of Jewish parent-
age, were on the margins of Jewish society and were of distinctly
inferior status. With the denial of table fellowship to the marginal
groups, they can be considered as having lost one of the markers identifying them as members of Jewish society.

Stratification of Jewish Society in the First Century CE. This discussion,
based primarily on first-century CE hellenistic Jewish sources, demonstrates that Jewish society in the first century CE was stratified. The
strata identified are depicted in table 5. Israelites were not discussed
above as a defined group because they constitute the norm against
which all other strata were measured. The statement in table 5 that
Israelites were permitted to marry proselytes is based on the fact that
marriage to an Israelite was one of the motivations for conversion to
Judaism.[166]

162. Philo, *Spec. Leg.* 1.102.
163. Josephus, *Ant.* 3.276; 4.245.
164. Cf. Josephus, *Ant.* 4.206.
165. *m. Qid.* 4.3.
166. Ilan, *Jewish Women*, p. 211.

Asymmetry and entitlement are present in this social structure. Access to four of the strata (Priests, Levites, Israelites, Proselytes) was determined by birth (birth and conversion in the case of the proselyte), and a fifth stratum (Blemished Priests) represented an irreversible lowering of status.

Stratification derived from first-century sources (table 5) is similar to that ordained by the Mishnah (table 4). Both schemes agree on the order: Priests, Levites, Israelites, Converts/Proselytes, Slaves, Marginal Groups. Further, the lists agree on marriageability as a major consideration in relating the strata to one another. Omissions in the lists, when compared with one another, are of little consequence to the issues under consideration here..

The only discrepancy between the lists is the status of impaired/ blemished priests. Josephus was not explicit in defining the marriageability of a blemished priest or his children, consequently an assignment of status based purely on marriageability might lower the status of the blemished priest. Alternatively, in the mishnaic regulation the connotations of 'impaired priest' may be more negative than Josephus's understanding of 'blemished' priests. However these variations are explained, Neusner's conclusion, that 'the whole [of the mishnaic stratification] derives from the second century',[167] is an overstatement. While some of the details may have originated in the second century, the stratification decreed by the Mishnah is very similar to the stratification described in the first century.

Assessing the Grid Status of First-Century CE Hellenistic Judaism

Grid strength in first-century CE hellenistic Judaism is evident in 'the cross-hatch of rules to which individuals [were] subject in the course of their interaction.'[168] These rules governed access and function in the central sanctuary of Jewish religion and the classes of people with whom marriage could be considered. Reinforcement of the grid occurred in the celebration of the holy days in the liturgical calendar and in the weekly participation in the life of the community/synagogue. The asymmetry and entitlement of the grid were supported by accountability in the form of synagogue-based punishment and the threat of execution for violation of the temple. All of these factors support the

---

167. Neusner, *The Mishnaic System of Women*, p. 175.
168. Douglas, 'Cultural Bias', p. 192.

conclusion that first-century CE hellenistic Judaism was a strong grid society.

Table 5. *Stratification of Jewish society according to first-century CE sources*

High Priests	nobility, permitted to marry the virgin daughter of a priest
Priests	nobility, permitted to marry the daughter of an Israelite
Blemished Priests	nobility (?)*, denied access to altar and Holy Place
Levites	the 'second rank' of the priest-hood
Israelites	permitted to marry proselytes
Proselytes	'Israelite' status in the third generation
Captives and Slaves	not suitable as mates for Israelites
Marginal Groups ('sinners and tax collectors')	denied table fellowship despite Jewish parentage

* The precise status of Blemished Priests is unclear. In the only mention of their status (Ant. 3.278), Josephus stated that they are entitled to 'their perquisites', but denied access to the altar and the ναός, 'central sanctuary'.

Based on the extant evidence, Greco-Roman authors demonstrated a relative lack of interest in the grid of Judaism. Far more evidence can be gleaned from Greco-Roman sources for assessing group strength than for grid strength. This discrepancy is probably a reflection of an outsider's greater interest in the external boundary of a society than in the interal structure of that society. Poised between Jewish and gentile worlds, the author of Luke–Acts was concerned about the structure of the society from which Christianity emerged; therefore, more reflections of grid are present in Luke–Acts than in the Greco-Roman sources.

The Group/Grid Status of Hellenistic Judaism

First-century CE hellenistic Judaism was a strong group, strong grid society within the larger Greco-Roman world. This conclusion is based on an examination of the writings of Josephus and Philo, supplemented by the outside perspectives of Greco-Roman authors, the transitional viewpoints of Paul and the author of Luke–Acts, and the relevant physical evidence (inscriptions and other archeological remains). The greatest limitation to the validity of this conclusion is the result of the substantial dependence on literary sources, which reflect preferentially a literate (i.e. high status) outlook. Factors mitigating this weakness are: (1) the inclusion of multiple perspectives in the analysis, and (2) the multi-faceted nature of the group identity and grid structure.

Chapter 3

GROUP/GRID ANALYSIS OF THE AUTHOR'S
IMPLIED SOCIETY

'Therefore, since we are receiving an unshakable kingdom, let us give thanks, by means of which we might serve God pleasingly with reverence and awe' (12.28). In this transition to the epistolary close of Hebrews, the author reminded the recipients that they had received an eschatological promise of membership in a secure kingdom, a realm more secure than, and, therefore, superior to, any society available outside the community of believers.

Elsewhere in the epistle, this ideal implied society is referred to as a city:

> He [Abraham] was waiting expectantly for the city having foundations, of which [city] the architect and builder is God (11.10).

> God is not ashamed to be called their God, for he prepared a city for them (11.16).

> You have approached Mount Zion, and the city of the living God, heavenly Jerusalem (12.22).

> We do not have here an abiding city, but we seek one that is coming (13.14).

To a first-century CE audience in the Roman Empire, the promise of a city was more than merely a promise of a place of residence. City life in the first-century was inherently social;[1] citizenship was a privilege and

1. Malina, *The New Testament World*, pp. 90-96; Richard L. Rohrbaugh, 'The Preindustrial City in Luke–Acts: Urban Social Relations', in Jerome H. Neyrey (ed.), *The Social World of Luke–Acts: Models for Interpretation* (Peabody, MA: Hendrickson, 1991), pp. 133-37; *idem*, 'The Preindustrial City', in Richard L. Rohrbaugh (ed.), *The Social Sciences and New Testament Interpretation* (Peabody, MA: Hendrickson, 1996), pp. 107-25 (118).

a significant component of a person's identity, and residence in a city was evidence of high status.

The city promised to the believing community can be described accurately as ideal, having been designed and built by God (11.10) for the believers (11.16). The apposition of the phrases 'city of the living God' and 'heavenly Jerusalem' (12.22) affirms the ideal nature of the promised home. In the final reference to the city, the believers are reassured that, though they lack a secure earthly city, that deficit will be remedied (13.14). With these comments, and the related reference to a 'homeland' (11.14), the author has invited the reader to inquire into the nature of the ideal implied society of believers.

Before commencing that inquiry, a comment on the nature of the evidence is necessary. Two forms of direct data and one form of indirect data are available. Hortatory subjunctives and imperatives calling for socially relevant behaviors and attitudes represent direct testimony by the author concerning the character of the implied society. Further direct testimony is available in the socially relevant behaviors and attitudes affirmed by the author, based on the assumption that affirmation implies approval. Finally, indirect testimony is present in Hebrews in the imagery and metaphors employed by the author (e.g. references to boundaries, kinship language, hierarchical language). Both direct and indirect data are assessed in the following group/grid analysis of the implied society.

Group Status of the Implied Society

Group Identity of the Congregation of Believers

The suggestion that the author viewed the gathering of believers in social, communal terms (based on the images of kingdom, city, and homeland noted above) is confirmed by the presence in the epistle of explicit kinship language. Four times the recipients are addressed with the vocative ἀδελφοί 'brothers'; (3.1, 12; 10.19; 13.22) and Timothy is described as 'our brother' (13.23). Establishment of these fictive kinship relationships was associated with the work of Jesus: 'For both the sanctifier and those being sanctified are all from one; for which reason he is not ashamed to call them brothers [and sisters]' (2.11). Such relationships were 'an extension of familiar loyalties...to others not related by blood, law, or other traditional ties' and were 'an integral part of the social structure of early Christianity.'[2]

Supplementing the fictive familial relationships uniting the believers into a community were the bonds of purpose, confession, and experience. Unity of purpose is evident in the designation of the recipients as 'partners [μέτοχοι] in a heavenly calling' (3.1), 'partners [μέτοχοι] of Christ' (3.14), and 'partners [κοινωνοί]' with those fellow believers suffering persecution (10.33). Moving from the indicative to the imperative, the author directed the believers to persist in brotherly love and to identify personally and intimately with imprisoned and suffering believers (13.1, 3).

Confession functions powerfully in reinforcing group identity; examples of this phenomenon include the climactic, fundamental nature of the *Shema* in Judaism and the Orthodox Christian devotion to the Nicene Creed without the *Filioque* clause.[3] Confessional vocabulary is prominent in Hebrews; the words ὁμολογέω, 'to confess' and ὁμολογία, 'confession' occur a total of five times.[4] Jesus is identified as the 'apostle and high priest of our confession' (3.1). Three occurrences are objects of hortatory subjunctives, the author appealing to the believers to hold fast to their confession (4.14; 10.23) and to voice their confession as worship to God (13.15). In two of the occurrences, the content of the confession is suggested: the exemplars of faithful living confessed 'that they were foreigners and strangers on the earth' (11.13) and

---

2.   Carolyn Osiek and David L. Balch, *Families in the New Testament World: Households and House Churches* (The Family, Religion, and Culture; Louisville: Westminster/John Knox Press, 1997), p. 54.

3.   Evelyn Garfiel, *Service of the Heart: A Guide to the Jewish Prayer Book* (Northvale, NJ: Jason Aronson, 1989), p. 85; Yitzchok Kirzner and Lisa Aiken, *The Art of Jewish Prayer* (Northvale, NJ: Jason Aronson, 1991), p. 30; Timothy Ware [Bishop Kallistos Ware], *The Orthodox Church* (Harmondsworth: Penguin Books, 3rd edn, 1993), pp. 50-51; *idem*, *The Orthodox Way* (Crestwood, NY: St. Vladimir's Seminary Press, 2nd edn, 1996), pp. 32, 92.

4.   This number of occurrences is comparable to that of 1 Jn, a document from a context where group identity was a critical issue. Throughout this study, concordance and frequency data are based on *Accordance*, computer software, ver. 2.1. (Altamonte Springs, FL: OakTree Software Specialists, 1996) and Philip S. Clapp, Barbara Friberg, and Timothy Friberg (eds.), *Analytical Concordance of the Greek New Testament*. I. *Lexical Focus* (Baker's Greek New Testament Library; Grand Rapids: Baker Book House, 1991).

the believers confess God's name (13:15).[5] Although confessions possess inherently a group defining power, Heb. 11.13 makes explicit the distinct identity of the confessing community.

The social function of common experience is implied in the first warning passage:

> Therefore we must attend more earnestly to *the things heard*, lest we be flowed past. For if the word spoken by angels was confirmed and every transgression and disobedience received the reward of a just punishment, how will we escape, having neglected so great a salvation, which *having been first spoken by the Lord, was confirmed to us by those who heard [him], God adding his testimony by signs and wonders and many kinds of powerful deeds and distributions of the Holy Spirit according to his will*? (2.1-4, emphasis mine).

The community's formative experiences are a basis for exhortation to future action. Similarly, in the fourth warning passage, the author cited more recent common experience to support his plea:

> *Remember the former days, after you were enlightened you endured a great struggle of suffering, sometimes being held up to derision with insults and affliction, sometimes becoming partners with those thus treated. For you also suffered together with the prisoners and you accepted with joy the plundering of your possessions*, because you know that you have better, abiding possessions. Therefore, do not cast away your boldness, which has a great reward. For you need endurance so that, after doing the will of God, you may receive the promise (10:32-36, emphasis mine).

Distinction between the Implied Society and First-Century CE Judaism

The author did not view the implied society as completely novel, for the founder of the community was the Creator (1.2). Precursors to the founding message were the messages of God through the prophets (1.1); therefore, the implied society and first-century CE Judaism shared

---

5.   The phrase τὸν ἀπόστολον καὶ ἀρχιερέα τῆς ὁμολογίας ἡμῶν Ἰησοῦν (Heb. 3.1) can be interpreted as 'we confess Jesus as apostle and high priest,' providing a third hint to the content of the community's confession; Harold W. Attridge, *The Epistle to the Hebrews* (Hermeneia; Philadelphia: Fortress Press, 1989), p. 108; cf. Paul Ellingworth, *The Epistle to the Hebrews: A Commentary on the Greek Text* (NIGTC; Grand Rapids: Eerdmans Publishing Company; Carlisle, UK: Paternoster Press, 1993), p. 199; Lane, *Hebrews 1–8*, p. 75.

a common heritage. This common heritage is evident in the author's references to 'the seed of Abraham' (2.16), in the description of the exemplars of faith under the former covenant as 'the elders' (11.2), and in the multitude of quotations from and allusions to the common scriptures of the Septuagint.

Despite the common heritage, the incarnation marked a disjunction. As described in the prologue to the epistle, the former communication from God is transcended 'in these last days' by the message borne by a son (1.1-2); the Son has replaced the Torah as the central symbol.[6] Faithfulness is a key element in the disjunction, resulting in a distinction between 'us' and 'them' (4.2).

Significant differentiation from first-century Judaism is evident in the transcendence of elements of Jewish identity. Not only has the Son replaced the Torah as central symbol, members of the implied society recognize that the law possesses 'a shadow of the good things to come, not the true form of those things' (10.1). Similarly, the covenant relating the community to God is 'better' than that enacted in the Torah (8.6), and the older covenant is 'near to vanishing' (8.13).

Sabbath observance, a prominent element of Jewish Torah praxis, is reinterpreted in the implied society. With his quotation of Gen. 2.2, the author transformed the Sabbath into an eschatological promise to the community, a promise denied to those who were disobedient with respect to the 'good news' (4.4-6).[7]

Kashrut and table fellowship were not immune from the author's attentions. Dietary rules were listed among the 'regulations of the flesh' that were in effect only 'until the time of setting right' (9.10), a time that arrived in the revelation of the Son.[8] Later in the epistle, kashrut regulations are compared unfavorably to the grace by which the believer's heart is sustained (13.9).[9] Redefinition of group membership, employing the metaphor of table fellowship, is suggested in Heb. 13.10: 'We have an altar from which those serving in the tabernacle do not

6.   Bruce Chilton and Jacob Neusner, *Judaism in the New Testament: Practices and Beliefs* (London: Routledge, 1995), pp. 183-84.

7.   Like the author of Hebrews, Josephus associated the Genesis account of creation with the institution of the Jewish Sabbath; *Ant.* 1.33.

8.   Ellingworth, *Hebrews*, p. 444.

9.   If the βρώμασιν to which the author referred in 13.9 were associated with festal meals, as is possible (Attridge, *Hebrews*, pp. 394-96), the transcendence of Jewish group definition includes the celebration of feasts and fasts.

have authority to eat.' According to this new definition, those thought most secure in their membership in the old group (i.e. the priestly nobility) have no such privilege in the new, implied society.

Devotion to the Jerusalem temple, a prominent characteristic of first-century CE hellenistic Judaism, is absent from the implied society. Shunning the terms ἱερόν, 'temple' and ναός, 'central sanctuary', the author couched his discussion in terms of the tabernacle. Peter Walker advanced the plausible hypothesis that this choice by the author reflected a decision 'not...to cast any aspersions on the contemporary Temple in practice,' preferring instead to make

> a far more fundamental point concerning the very essence of the Temple. By concentrating his attention on the 'tabernacle' in the wilderness, he could argue that the Tabernacle system of worship, even when considered in its most pristine and pure form under Moses (before any human sin might have twisted the divine intention), had been declared redundant by God through Jesus.[10]

Such a transcendence of the first-century Jewish perspective is evident in the contrast between the 'earthly sanctuary' (9.1) and the 'greater and more perfect tabernacle' in which Jesus offered his sacrifice 'once for all' (9.11-12).

Group Strength of the Implied Society

Boundaries in Hebrews. Having demonstrated that the author viewed the congregation in societal terms and that the implied society stood in relation to, yet distinct from, first-century CE hellenistic Judaism, application of Douglas's group/grid paradigm is legitimate. Lacking explicit declarations of the group strength of the implied society, an examination of the author's use of boundary imagery provides a means of assessing this parameter. Douglas's definition of group 'in terms of the claims it makes over its constituent members, *the boundary it draws around them*, the rights it confers on them to use its name and other protections, and the levies and constraints it applies' (emphasis mine)[11] offers sanction for this indirect procedure for establishing group strength in the implied society.

The clearest example of boundary imagery in Hebrews occurs near the conclusion of the epistle.

---

10. Peter W.L. Walker, *Jesus and the Holy City: New Testament Perspectives on Jerusalem* (Grand Rapids: Eerdmans, 1996), pp. 207-208.

11. Douglas, 'Cultural Bias', p. 191.

> For the animals whose blood is carried into the sanctuary by the high
> priest as a sin offering, their bodies are burned outside the camp. There-
> fore [διὸ], Jesus also suffered outside the gate in order to sanctify the
> people with his own blood. Therefore [τοίνυν], let us go out to him, out-
> side the camp, bearing his reproach; for we do not have here an abiding
> city, but we seek one that is coming (13.11-14).

In the crucifixion of Jesus outside the city gates of Jerusalem, the author
found a parallel to the disposal of the bodies of the Yom Kippur
sacrificial victims.

This levitical prescription (Lev. 16.27), coupled with the ritual
expulsion of the scapegoat (Lev. 16.22) and with the requirements for
cleansing before returning to the camp (Lev. 16.26, 28), presumes a
clear distinction between sacred space (within the camp) and profane
space (outside the camp); therefore, the perimeter of the camp is a conspicuous boundary. In the first century CE the walls of Jerusalem were
invested with the same function as the camp perimeter: outside the
walls was the appropriate place for the execution of prisoners.[12]
According to the Mishnah, though Jerusalem was the holiest of all
cities, all walled cities possessed an enhanced status. 'The cities sur-
rounded by a wall are more holy than it [the land]. For they send from
them the lepers, and they carry around in their midst a corpse so long as
they like. [But once] it has gone forth, they do not bring it back. Within
the wall [of Jerusalem] is more holy than they. For they eat there lesser
sanctities and second tithe.'[13]

Moving into the Greco-Roman world, a similar attitude toward city
walls is encountered. Recalling the legendary origins of Rome, Plutarch
wrote:

> Romulus...set himself to building his city, after summoning from
> Tuscany men who prescribed all the details in accordance with certain
> sacred ordinances and writings, and taught them to him as in a religious
> rite... Then, taking this as a centre, they marked out the city in a circle
> round it. And the founder, having shod a plough with a brazen
> ploughshare, and having yoked to it a bull and a cow, himself drove a
> deep furrow round the boundary lines, while those who followed after
> him had to turn the clods, which the plough threw up, inwards toward the

---

12. Josephus, *War* 4.360; *idem*, *Ant.* 4.264; Acts 7.58. The similarity of wording
is worth noting: ἔξω τῶν πυλῶν (*War* 4.360), ἔξω τῆς πόλεως (*Ant.* 4.264), ἔξω τῆς
πόλεως (Acts 7.58), ἔξω τῆς παρεμβολῆς...ἔξω τῆς πύλης...ἔξω τῆς παρεμβολῆς
(Heb. 13.11-13); cf. ἔξω τῆς παρεμβολῆς (Lev. 16.27 LXX).

13. *m. Kel.* 1.7-8.

city, and suffer no clod to lie turned outwards. With this line they mark out the course of the wall, and it is called, by contraction, 'pomerium,' that is 'post murum,' *behind* or *next the wall.* And where they purposed to put in a gate, there they took the share out of the ground, lifted the plough over, and left a vacant space. And this is the reason why they regard all the wall as sacred except the gates; but if they held all the gates as sacred, it would not be possible, without religious scruples, to bring into and send out of the city things which are necessary, and yet unclean.[14]

Varro described a similar ritual employed in the founding of other Latin towns, commenting that 'for reasons of religion they did this on an auspicious day.'[15] This Roman attitude toward city walls, combined with the comparable Jewish perspective, suggests that first-century hellenistic Jews residing in the Roman Empire would have viewed city walls as significant boundaries.

In this social context, by mentioning Jesus' execution 'outside the gate' (13.12) and by exhorting the recipients to 'go out to him, outside the camp' (13.13), the author of Hebrews was employing emphatic boundary crossing language. This emphasis is magnified by the author's repetitive use of the phrases ἔξω τῆς παρεμβολῆς ('outside the camp'), ἔξω τῆς πύλης ('outside the gate'), ἔξω τῆς παρεμβολῆς ('outside the camp') (13.11-13),[16] particularly in the third instance where the prepositional phrase is somewhat redundant; the exhortation ἐξερχώμεθα πρὸς αὐτὸν ('let us go out to him'), would have been adequate to convey the message. By associating this boundary crossing imagery with the believers' anticipated, eschatological city (13.14), the author implied that this permeable boundary is characteristic of the implied society; therefore, that society is open to interaction with outsiders.

Confronted with such explicit language, George Wesley Buchanan attributed Heb. 13 to an 'annotator'.[17] This distancing of the final chapter from the remainder of the epistle was necessary, in part, because of Buchanan's hypothesis that 'the readers belonged to a very strict, communal, monastic sect' and that the author 'may have been one of the leaders of a Christian monastery in Jerusalem to which these migrants

14. Plutarch, *Lives, Romulus* 11. Livy (*History of Rome* 1.7.2-3) noted the construction of city walls as one of Romulus's first acts in the founding of Rome.

15. Varro, *De Lingua Latina* 5.143.

16. Cf. Ellingworth, *Hebrews*, p. 714.

17. George Wesley Buchanan, *To the Hebrews: A New Translation with Introduction and Commentary* (AB; New York: Doubleday, 1972), p. 235.

had come.'[18] That such a sectarian would not have employed the boundary crossing language of Heb. 13.11-13 is reflected in Buchanan's statement that the annotator 'was not a monk'.[19]

The issue of the unity of Hebrews is beyond the scope of the present study. Lacking any manuscript evidence for a conflation of an original homily (Heb. 1–12) and a later epistolary appendix (Heb. 13), the unity of Hebrews has been assumed in this work.[20] Buchanan's treatment of Heb. 13 does, however, provide a measure of confirmation for the interpretation advanced here, namely that the exhortation of Heb. 13.13 suggests an implied society that is open to interaction with outsiders. That confirmation comes in the fact that, having reached a conclusion on the purpose of Hebrews that is contrary to the thesis of the present research, Buchanan was compelled to excise the final chapter from the homily.

DeSilva, another interpreter who read Hebrews as a sectarian document,[21] has devoted some attention to the interpretation of Heb. 13.13. He commented that 'the addressees will be urged to join in this movement away from at-homeness within society near the end of the exhortation (13.12-14).'[22] Here, as elsewhere, deSilva focussed on the origin and destination of the pilgrims or on issues of honor and shame,[23] never on the boundary being crossed. By not addressing the boundary crossing language, deSilva omitted any explanation of how such imagery could be employed by a sectarian.

Attridge noted in Heb. 13.13 a recollection of 'other appeals to movement in Hebrews. Yet the imagery has shifted. Where previous appeals had called for entry (4.11)…the present appeal is for movement in the opposite direction.'[24] In that earlier entreaty, the author urged the

---

18. Buchanan, *To the Hebrews*, pp. 256, 264.

19. Buchanan, *To the Hebrews*, p. 267.

20. For an argument in support of the integrity of Heb. 1–13, see Lane, *Hebrews 1–8*, pp. lxvii-lxviii and Floyd V. Filson, *'Yesterday': A Study of Hebrews in the Light of Chapter 13* (SBT; London: SCM Press, 1967), pp. 82-83.

21. deSilva, 'The Epistle to the Hebrews in Social-Scientific Perspective', pp. 1-21 passim.

22. deSilva, *Despising Shame*, p. 200. Note that though deSilva viewed the author as a sectarian, he did not dispute the integrity of the canonical form of Hebrews.

23. deSilva, *Despising Shame*, pp. 6-8, 194, 206, 208, 312; *idem*, 'Despising Shame', pp. 449, 458.

24. Attridge, *Hebrews*, p. 398.

recipients to 'be diligent to enter into that rest, so that no one may fall into that same example of disobedience' (4:11). This plea comes at the conclusion of a midrash on Ps. 95, a text that recalls the disobedience of the wilderness generation. Although the rebellion at Kadesh-barnea is not mentioned explicitly in Ps. 95 or in Hebrews, the forty-year wandering is noted explicitly (Ps. 95.10 [LXX 94.10]; Heb. 3.10) as is the divine oath that the disobedient generation would not enter the promised land (Ps. 95.11 [LXX 94.11]; Heb. 3.11). The disobedience recalled in the psalm does, therefore, include the rebellion at Kadesh-barnea. With the author's repeated references to the 40 years and to the oath (3.17-18; 4.3, 5), combined with his additional comment on the corpses that fell in the wilderness (ὧν τὰ κῶλα ἔπεσεν ἐν τῇ ἐρήμῳ ['whose corpses fell in the wilderness'], 3.17; an allusion to Num. 14.29, 32 ἐν τῇ ἐρήμῳ ταύτῃ πεσεῖται τὰ κῶλα ὑμῶν...καὶ τὰ κῶλα ὑμῶν πεσεῖται ἐν τῇ ἐρήμῳ ταύτῃ LXX ['in this wilderness your corpses will fall...and your corpses will fall in this wilderness']), clearly the author included the rebellion at Kadesh-barnea in the disobedience of the wilderness generation.[25]

While Attridge is correct in stating that Heb. 4.11 calls for entry whereas Heb. 13.13 appeals for an exit, there is a fundamental similarity between the exhortations. The disobedience to which the author referred in Heb. 4.11 was a refusal to cross a boundary (from the wilderness to the land of promised rest). The exhortation in Heb. 4.11 is to cross that boundary, now viewed in metaphorical terms (as the author demonstrated by his reference to Joshua; Heb. 4.8); therefore, both Heb. 4.14 and Heb. 13.13 appeal for the crossing of a boundary. Any attempt to equate the motion as movement from the sacred to the profane falters; in Heb. 4.11 the motion is into the 'holy' land but in Heb. 13.13 the motion is from the sacred space of the city to the profane space beyond the walls.[26]

Reinforcement of the significance of boundary crossing is evident in another historical connection to Ps. 95/Heb. 3–4. After the extended quotation from the psalm in Heb. 3.7-11, the author mentioned the

25. Cf. Paul Ellingworth and Eugene Albert Nida, *A Handbook on the Letter to the Hebrews* (UBS Handbook Series; New York: United Bible Societies, 1983), p. 82.

26. Alternatively, the author may have redefined sacred space as 'where Jesus is'; cf. L. Paul Trudinger, 'The Gospel Meaning of the Secular: Reflections on Hebrews 13:10-13', *EvQ* 54 (1982), pp. 235-37.

divine wrath and oath in Heb. 3.17-18, repeated the quotation of the relevant verse from the psalm in Heb. 4.3, and repeated the content of the oath again in Heb. 4.5. Mention of the divine wrath and oath occur in Num. 32.10-13 as a response to the request by the trans-Jordan tribes to remain on the west side of the river, a request for exemption from crossing a boundary. The threat is lifted only when the able-bodied men of these tribes consent to cross the river/boundary as a vanguard for the Israelite forces (Num. 32.16-24).

In footnotes, Attridge identified other examples of movement reminiscent of that described in Heb. 13.13:

> Therefore, let us approach the throne of grace with boldness, in order that we might receive mercy and might find grace for timely help (4.16).

> which we have as an anchor of the soul, secure and firm and entering into the inside of the curtain, where Jesus entered for us as a forerunner, having become a high priest forever according to the order of Melchizedek (6.19-20)

> [N]ot by the blood of goats and calves but by his own blood he entered once for all into the sanctuary, eternal redemption having been secured (9.12).

> For Christ did not enter into the handmade sanctuary, which is a copy of the true one, but into heaven itself, now appearing in the presence of God for us (9.24).

> [L]et us approach with true hearts in full assurance of faith, hearts having been sprinkled from an evil conscience and bodies having been washed with pure water (10.22).[27]

Each of these examples refers (either explicitly or by allusion) to an entrance into the Holy of Holies.

In the first case noted by Attridge, the 'throne of grace' is the heavenly reality of which the earthly Holy of Holies was a copy,[28] and now the believer is able to 'approach...with boldness.' With the mention of 'inside the curtain' in the second example the allusion to the earthly Holy of Holies is more explicit, and the description of Jesus as a 'forerunner' implies that the believers will follow.[29] According to the

---

27. Attridge, *Hebrews*, p. 398 nn. 117, 118.

28. F.F. Bruce, *The Epistle to the Hebrews* (NICNT; Grand Rapids: Eerdmans, 2nd edn, 1990), p. 116; cf. Lane, *Hebrews 1–8*, p. 115.

29. James Moffatt, *A Critical and Exegetical Commentary on the Epistle to the Hebrews* (ICC; Edinburgh: T. & T. Clark, 1924), pp. 89-90; cf. Buchanan, *To the*

levitical cult, the only requirement for bringing blood into the central sanctuary was to complete the Yom Kippur sacrifices; therefore, Heb. 9.12 contains another reference to Christ's entry into the Holy of Holies.[30] Christ's entry into heaven is presented as a more intimate approach to God than any entry into an earthly sanctuary, and the subsequent mention of the high priest's entry 'every year with the blood of another' (9.25) confirms that Christ has entered into a greater Holy of Holies.[31] The believers' approach mentioned in the final example cited by Attridge is possible by 'a new and living way through the curtain, that is his [Jesus'] flesh, having been inaugurated' (10.20); again the author has alluded to the Holy of Holies.[32]

The cumulative effect of these statements is to demonstrate that the author exhorted the believers to cross the boundary into the true Holy of Holies following the example of Christ, a transit made possible by Christ's self-sacrifice. With this appeal, the most protected boundary in first-century CE Judaism has (metaphorically) been crossed.

As noted in the above discussion, Jesus' entry into the heavenly Holy of Holies prepared the way for believers to follow. This transit by Jesus from earth to heaven is itself another example of a boundary crossing. Philo noted the existence of a boundary separating the divine presence in heaven from the earth, describing this world (κόσμος) as 'the gate...of heaven' (πύλην τοῦ...οὐρανοῦ),[33] suggesting that the word οὐρανός was derived from ὅρος (boundary),[34] and finding in the tabernacle furnishings a symbolic representation of the bounding of the material world by heaven.[35] Jesus, whose incarnation is described explicitly in Hebrews (in the sharing of flesh and blood; 2.14), entered into 'heaven itself' (εἰς αὐτὸν τὸν οὐρανόν, 9.24) to appear before God, and was even described as 'having become higher than the heavens' (ὑψηλότερος τῶν οὐρανῶν γενόμενος, 7.26). In the exaltation of

Hebrews, p. 116; Bruce, *Hebrews*, p. 155; Lane, *Hebrews 1–8*, p. 154.

30. Cf. Ellingworth, *Hebrews*, p. 452; Attridge, *Hebrews*, p. 248; Bruce, *Hebrews*, p. 213; Buchanan, *To the Hebrews*, pp. 147-48.

31. Attridge, *Hebrews*, p. 262-64; cf. Ellingworth, *Hebrews*, p. 479-80; William L. Lane, *Hebrews 9–13* (WBC; Dallas: Word Books, 1991), pp. 248-49.

32. Bruce, *Hebrews*, pp. 250-51; cf. Buchanan, *To the Hebrews*, p. 168; Ellingworth, *Hebrews*, p. 520; Attridge, *Hebrews*, pp. 284-85.

33. Philo, *Somn.* 1.185-187.

34. Philo, *Op. Mund.* 37.

35. Philo, *Rer. Div. Her.* 227-28.

the Son, the supreme cosmological boundary was crossed by the 'fore-runner'.

In the final warning passage in Hebrews, the author presented a stark contrast:

> For you have not approached something tangible and burning with fire and with darkness and gloom and tempest and with the sound of a trumpet and with a voice whose utterances caused those who heard to beg that not another word be added to them, for they could not bear the command, 'And if a beast touches the mountain, it will be stoned'; and, so fearful was the appearance, Moses said, 'Terrified am I, and trembling'. Rather, you have approached Mount Zion, and the city of the living God, heavenly Jerusalem, and myriads of angels in festal gathering, and the assembly [ἐκκλησία] of the firstborn who have been enrolled in heaven, and God who is the judge of all, and the spirits of the righteous who have been perfected, and Jesus, the mediator of a new covenant, and the sprinkled blood that speaks better than that of Abel (12.18-24).

The description of the 'tangible' mountain is drawn from the accounts of the Mt Sinai theophany (Exod. 19.12-25; 20.18-21; Deut. 4.11-12; 5.22-27; 9.19). A significant aspect of that event, as recalled by the author, was the strictly-enforced boundary separating the people and their herds and flocks from the divine presence. That theophany, under the former covenant, is contrasted with a new covenant theophany, and the description of the second mountain implies access.

Based on other references to 'city' in Hebrews, the identification of Mt Zion as 'the city of the living God' can be viewed as an invitation rather than a prohibition. Previously the author commented that God had prepared a city for the faithful (11.16), and later in the epistle the author exclaimed that believers seek a city that is coming (13.14). With these expressions of citizenship and expectation, the natural conclusion is that believers may cross the threshold of Mt Zion without fear of divine retribution. With the invitation to enter the true Holy of Holies, noted above, the gates of the 'city of the living God' would be assumed to be open to the faithful. Mention of 'the assembly of the firstborn who have been enrolled in heaven' confirms the conclusion that believers have full access to this mountain.[36] The significance of this openness is enhanced with the recognition that the contrast presented by the author

---

36. Lane, *Hebrews 9–13*, pp. 464-68; cf. Thomas G. Long, *Hebrews* (Int, Louisville: John Knox Press, 1997), p. 138; Bruce, *Hebrews*, pp. 357-59.

is between a vision of the implied society and the foundational event of Judaism.

As with the other examples encountered in Hebrews, the faithful are invited to cross the boundary. No impenetrable boundaries exist in the implied society; for the faithful all boundaries are permeable. Such consistency in the employment of boundary imagery in Hebrews suggests that the author did not envision the implied society as strong group. In Hebrews boundaries are not to be avoided or defended, but crossed; therefore, the implied society should be viewed as weak group.

Returning to the Day of Atonement analogies employed by the author, one aspect of the liturgy is absent from the discussion in Hebrews: the expulsion of the scapegoat (Lev. 16.22). Although this event is a boundary crossing, this crossing reinforces the boundary by transmitting the contagion to the wilderness and restoring the purity of the camp. The author's silence on the scapegoat can be explained, in part, as a result of the boundary reinforcing character of the expulsion.

As is implied in this comment about the scapegoat, one category of boundaries has not been addressed in the above discussion: purity boundaries. This silence reflects the absence from Hebrews of references to purity boundaries, separating the 'clean' from the 'unclean'. Purity has, rather, been redefined in Hebrews; consequently, the discussion of purity must be postponed until the cosmology of Hebrews is addressed in the next chapter.[37]

Other Indicators of Group Strength in Hebrews. Confirmation of the weak group status of the implied society comes in the paraenesis with which the author introduced the conclusion of the epistle. 'Let brotherly love abide. Do not forget to show hospitality to strangers, for by this means some unknowingly entertained angels' (13.1-2). With the first imperative group identity is reinforced through φιλαδελφία. In contrast, the second imperative reaches beyond group boundaries with φιλοξενία. Whereas φιλαδελφία involves 'affection for one's fellow believer in Christ', to demonstrate φιλοξενία is 'to receive and show hospitality to a stranger, that is, someone who is not regarded as a member of the extended family or a close friend.'[38] Some commentators have

37. Redefinition of purity is another possible explanation for the author's silence about the scapegoat.

38. Johannes P. Louw and Eugene A. Nida (eds.), *Greek English Lexicon of the New Testament Based on Semantic Domains*. I. *Introduction and Domains* (New

concluded that the objects of φιλοξενία were itinerant Christians who were not members of the recipient congregation(s), though Paul Ellingworth admitted that 'this is not emphasized'.[39] Such a limitation on hospitality would not, however, demonstrate that the implied society is strong group. A minimalist interpretation of Heb. 13.2 includes the imperative to welcome those not immediately recognized as members of the congregation, to refrain from suspicion in interaction with newly acquainted believers; such attitudes are weak group responses.

Nationalistic language can serve as a strong group indicator. Such language is lacking in Hebrews. As was discussed above, the author did understand the community of believers to be the legitimate descendants of the faithful under the former covenant, but he refrained from employing national language to describe the new community. The terms Ἑβραῖος, Ἰουδαῖος, ἔθνος ('Hebrew, Jew/Judean, gentile') and their cognates are absent. The only potentially nationalistic terms employed in Hebrews are Ἰσραήλ ('Israel') (8.8, 10; 11.22) and Ἰούδας ('Judah') (7.14; 8.8). The earlier occurrence of Ἰούδας is in an admission that Jesus lacked a priestly genealogy, and the last occurrence of Ἰσραήλ is a reference to the exodus from Egypt, not to the implied society. The other three occurrences of these terms are in the quotation of the new covenant passage from Jeremiah. Any ambiguity about the nationalistic significance of this quotation is resolved by the author's repetition of a portion of the Jeremiah text in Heb. 10.16-17. In that repetition the author substituted πρὸς αὐτούς ('with them') (10.16) for τῷ οἴκῳ Ἰσραήλ ('with the house of Israel') (8.10). The probable explanation for the substitution is that the author sought to emphasize the 'more universal scope' of the new covenant,[40] thereby moving toward a weaker group status.[41]

York: United Bible Societies, 2nd edn, 1989), pp. 293, 454-55; §25.34; 34.57.

39. Ellingworth, *Hebrews*, p. 694; cf. Bruce, *Hebrews*, p. 370; Buchanan, *To the Hebrews*, p. 230.

40. Attridge, *Hebrews*, p. 281. Although Ellingworth (*Hebrews*, p. 513) stated that the modification simplified the application of 'the text to readers some of whom may be gentiles', he denied that the change 'denationalizes' the quotation. Even if the latter statement is conceded, the admission of gentiles into the new covenant is not a strong group response with respect to first-century CE hellenistic Judaism.

41. The absence of ethnic/nationalistic language in Hebrews can be contrasted with the presence of such expressions in the Pauline epistles (Rom. 1.16; 3.29; 9.24; 1 Cor. 12.13; Gal. 2.14; 3.28) and in Luke–Acts (Acts 14.1, 5; 18.4; 19.10, 17; 20.21). Note particularly Paul's exclamation: πᾶς Ἰσραὴλ σωθήσεται (Rom. 11.26).

In a detailed examination of Heb. 11, Pamela Michelle Eisenbaum reached the same conclusion about the non-nationalistic nature of the rhetoric of Hebrews. Introducing her thesis, she stated: 'Hebrews' reading of the great heroes and events of biblical history serves both to *denationalize* Jewish scripture and to re-value the religious significance of Jewish history so that its ethnic peculiarity is rendered inconsequential' (emphasis original).[42] A noteworthy example of this tendency is the description of Moses. According to the author, Moses identified with the 'people of God' (τῷ λαῷ τοῦ θεοῦ) Heb. 11.25, removing the nationalistic overtones in the apparent parallel in the LXX where Moses identified with 'the sons of Israel' (τοὺς υἱοὺς Ισραηλ, Exod. 2.11). At the conclusion of her study, Eisenbaum stated that the non-nationalistic thrust of Heb. 11 was intentional; 'the author's purpose is to denationalize the history of Israel'.[43]

Descriptions of those who are 'inside' and those who are 'outside' with respect to group membership serve as another indicator of group strength. Outsiders are mentioned in Hebrews, twice as 'enemies' (ἐχθροὶ, 1.13; 10.13), twice as 'sinners' (ἁμαρτωλοὶ, 7.26; 12.3), and once as 'adversaries' (ὑπεναντίοι, 10.27). 'Enemies' are identified based on their relationship to Jesus. The first occurrence emphasizes the exalted status of the Son, quoting Ps. 110.1 (LXX 109.1):

> To which of the angels has he ever said,
> > Sit at my right hand
> > > until I place your enemies as a footstool for your feet? (1.13).

An echo of this quotation occurs later in the epistle: 'And every priest stands daily ministering again the same sacrifices many times, which are never able to remove sins, but this one, having offered one sacrifice for sins, forever sat down at the right hand of God, henceforth waiting expectantly until his enemies be placed as a footstool for his feet' (10.11-13). Although enmity with Jesus implies outsider status, that status is not emphasized with respect to distinction from the believers.

As is the case in Heb. 10.13, Jesus' status as high priest is the context for one of the references to 'sinners':

> For indeed such a high priest was appropriate for us, pious, without evil, undefiled, having been separated from sinners and having become higher

---

42. Pamela Michelle Eisenbaum, *The Jewish Heroes of Christian History: Hebrews 11 in Literary Context* (SBLDS, 156; Atlanta: Scholars Press, 1997), p. 3.

43. Eisenbaum, *The Jewish Heroes of Christian History*, p. 188.

than the heavens, who does not need daily, as do the high priests, to offer sacrifices first for his own sins, then for those of the people; for this he did once for all when he offered himself (7.26-27).

Two interpretations for the phrase 'having been separated from sinners' have been advanced. According to one view the separation reflects the high priestly requirement for the Day of Atonement, when the high priest resided in the temple for the week preceding the annual sacrifice.[44] A second interpretation associates 'having been separated from sinners' with the following phrase, 'having become higher than the heavens', and equates the separation with the ascension, in which Jesus was separated from all humanity.[45] In both cases, the separation is not specifically from outsiders, but from all humanity. In the priestly interpretation, that separation excludes explicitly other Jews, other members of the group. This reference to 'sinners' does not, therefore, distinguish clearly between insiders and outsiders with respect to the implied society.

The 'adversaries' are identified as objects of divine wrath: 'For if we are sinning deliberately after receiving the knowledge of truth, a sacrifice for sins no longer remains, but some fearful expectation of judgement and zealous fire about to consume the adversaries' (10.26-27). In a manner similar to the occurrences of ἐχθροί ('enemies'), here the adversaries are identified based on their status before God, not primarily on their exclusion from the implied society.

Only with the second reference to 'sinners' did the author approach a contrast between outsiders and insiders: 'for consider him who has endured such hostility from sinners against himself, in order that, growing faint, your souls may not become weary' (12.3). Again, the outsiders are identified based on their relationship to Jesus, but a possible extension of the contrast comes in the next sentence: 'Not yet have you resisted to the point of shedding blood, you who struggle against sin' (12.4). With the transition from the mention of the crucifixion to the implied anticipation of persecution directed against believers, the equation of 'sinners' with those excluded from the community is conceivable.[46] If the author intended such an extension of the contrast, he did

44. Buchanan, *To the Hebrews*, p. 128; Attridge, *Hebrews*, p. 213; Bruce, *Hebrews*, p. 176 n. 88. Both Buchanan and Attridge cited *m. Yom.* 1.1 as evidence. Ellingworth (*Hebrews*, p. 394) considered this interpretation 'unlikely.'

45. Lane, *Hebrews 1–8*, p. 192; Moffatt, *Hebrews*, pp. 101-102; Ellingworth and Nida, *The Letter to the Hebrews*, p. 159.

46. Cf. Bruce, *Hebrews*, p. 342; Lane, *Hebrews 9–13*, p. 417.

not make that point explicit. Rather, he stated that the believers' struggle was against 'sin', not against 'sinners' (πρὸς τὴν ἁμαρτίαν not πρὸς τοὺς ἁμαρτωλούς).[47]

In all of these instances of possible outsider language, the contrast between the outsiders and the believers has been implicit, if present at all. Apparently, the author was not concerned to identify outsiders as opponents of the believers, but to identify outsiders as foes of God. Such lack of concern to emphasize the outsiders as opponents to the community of believers is suggested in the author's reference to earlier instances of suffering:

> Remember the former days, after you were enlightened you endured a great struggle of suffering, sometimes being held up to derision with insults and affliction, sometimes becoming partners with those thus treated. For you also suffered together with the prisoners and you accepted with joy the plundering of your possessions, because you know that you have better, abiding possessions (10.32-34).

Here the events are mentioned without identifying the persons engaged in the assault on the believers; the author's attention was on the faithful endurance of the believers, not on identifying those who are outside the faithful community.[48]

A reversal of outsider language occurs in the author's use of the adjective ἀλλότριος ('foreign'). In Heb. 11.34 the meaning is 'foreign', describing the armies defeated by the faithful predecessors. Earlier in the same chapter Abraham and the other patriarchs are described as residing εἰς γῆν...ἀλλοτρίαν ('in a foreign land') (11.9); to the archetypal 'insiders' is ascribed the status of 'aliens'. Eisenbaum noted that 'Jewish exegetical traditions avoid or ignore the fact that Abraham is not truly an Israelite.'[49] In this environment, the author's boldness in marginalizing *the* patriarch is exceptional. Conversely, the author was silent about the inhabitants of the land, minimizing potential strong group implications of the patriarchs' alien status; his intent was to describe the exemplars as faithful pilgrims seeking God's promises (cf.

---

47. Cf. Attridge, *Hebrews*, p. 360.

48. One possible description of outsiders is the string of participles in Heb. 6.4-6. Though difficulties of interpretation limit the usefulness of this description, if the persons being described are to be viewed as outsiders, their status is self-imposed and is based on their response to 'the Son of God'. Neither excommunication by nor exclusion from the community is addressed.

49. Eisenbaum, *The Jewish Heroes of Christian History*, p. 156.

the similar use of ξένος ('strange/foreign') in Heb. 11.13[50]), not to establish a national barrier between the faithful and those outside the community.

All of the evidence in Hebrews suggests that the author envisioned the implied society as weak group with respect to first-century CE hellenistic Judaism. The imperative τῆς φιλοξενίας μὴ ἐπιλανθάνεσθε (13.2), the shunning of nationalistic language, and the apparent reluctance to employ 'insider versus outsider' rhetoric all point to this conclusion, a conclusion reached independently by the consideration of boundary imagery in the epistle.

The only clear distinction between 'insiders' and 'outsiders' is based on the person's response to God's redemptive work through the Son. Exclusion from the group is, therefore, based on the will of the outsider, not on a prohibition by insiders. Though the issue is never addressed by the author, presumably the outsider can cross the boundary into the community through a change of heart with respect to God.

Admittedly, two of the points noted (lack of nationalistic language and lack of 'insider versus outsider' rhetoric) are arguments from silence, but the silences are conspicuous. The paraphrasing of the new covenant passage to remove the title 'Israel' and the failure to name the persecutors, even when the previous sentence had identified 'sinners' as Jesus' opponents, suggest that the author's lack of strong group language is conscious and intentional. Repeating the conclusion stated above, the implied society should be viewed as weak group.

Grid Status of the Implied Society

Recalling Douglas's definitions, grid consists of 'rules which relate one person to others on an ego-centered basis,' 'visible rules about space and time related to social roles.'[51] Because the group/grid paradigm is a comparative model, establishing the grid status of the implied society involves both establishing the internal structure of that society and comparing and contrasting the grid of the implied society to the grid of first-century Judaism.

50. Eisenbaum (*The Jewish Heroes of Christian History*, p. 161 n. 102) noted that in Heb. 11.13 'the author of Hebrews has substituted the stronger ξένοι for πάροικος', the latter word occurring in Gen. 23.4, the LXX text to which the author was alluding.

51. Douglas, *Natural Symbols*, p. viii; *idem*, 'Cultural Bias', p. 192.

The Structure of the Implied Society

The Status of the Son in the Implied Society. Unambiguously, the superior position in the structure of the implied society is occupied by the Son. Daniel Ebert identified a centered chiasm in the prologue of Hebrews.[52] At the central (D) position of the chiasm is the declaration, 'who being the radiance of his glory and the exact representation of his nature, and upholding all things by his powerful word' (1.3), phrases emphasizing the intimate relationship between God and the Son. One of the following statements in the prologue (B') announces that the Son 'sat down at the right hand of the majesty on high' (1.3). Four further times in the epistle this heavenly session is mentioned:

> To which of the angels has he ever said,
> > Sit at my right [hand]
> > > until I place your enemies as a footstool for your feet? (1.13)

> [W]e have such a high priest, who sat down at the right [hand] of the throne of the majesty in the heavens (8.1).

> [T]his one, having offered one sacrifice for sins, forever sat down at the right [hand] of God (10.12).

> the pioneer and perfecter of the faith, Jesus, who for the sake of the joy that lay before him endured the cross, despising the shame, and has sat down at the right [hand] of the throne of God (12.2)

In each mention of the Son's heavenly enthronement the location is identified explicitly as the 'right [hand]' of God, the position of highest status.[53] Further enhancing Jesus' station is the longevity of his reign: 'forever' (10.12).[54]

Additional evidence of Jesus' exalted status in the implied society is the title applied frequently to him: high priest. On ten occasions, the author referred to Jesus as ἀρχιερεὺς (2.17; 3.1; 4.14, 15; 5.5, 10; 6.20; 7.26; 8.1; 9.11). This title is included in the author's summary of the

---

52. Daniel J. Ebert, 'The Chiastic Structure of the Prologue to Hebrews', *Trinity Journal* 13 (1992), pp. 163-79 (167).

53. Louw and Nida, *Greek-English Lexicon*, p. 737; §87.34, 36. The superlative nature of the Son's status is based on the person on whose right hand he is placed: God.

54. The author's use of the phrase εἰς τὸ διηνεκὲς in Heb. 10.12 is ambiguous. For the reasons stated by Ellingworth and Nida (*The Letter to the Hebrews*, p. 223), the phrase has been assumed to modify the following clause, ἐκάθισεν ἐν δεξιᾷ τοῦ θεοῦ.

'main point' (κεφάλαιον) of the discussion of Jesus and Melchizedek (8.1). The Son is a more suitable high priest than those who minister in the earthly sanctuary because, unlike them, Jesus 'does not need daily, as do the high priests, to offer sacrifices first for his own sins, then for those of the people; for this he did once for all when he offered himself' (7.27). Like his heavenly reign, Jesus' ministry as high priest is 'forever' (εἰς τὸν αἰῶνα; 6.20); a duration denied to other priests (7.23-24). Jesus is the unchallenged eternal head of the implied society.

The relationship between the Son and believers is made explicit in Heb. 3.6: 'Christ [is faithful] as a son over his [God's] house, of whom we ourselves are the house, if indeed we hold fast to the boldness and the boast of hope.' This image of Jesus 'over' believers is consistent with an implied comparison in the epistle. Based largely on their access to God, including access to the true Holy of Holies (4.16; 10.22), John Scholer described the believers as possessing 'priestly status', or, in anticipation of the eschaton, as 'proleptic priests'.[55] Granted this status, believers are, therefore, related, yet subordinate, to the Son as priests to the high priest.

Another aspect of the association between the Son and believers is revealed in the author's allusions to the incarnation and his related use of kinship language. While maintaining the distinction between Jesus (as 'sanctifier') and the believers (as the 'sanctified'), the author noted the family relationship: 'For both the sanctifier and those being sanctified are all from one; for which reason he is not ashamed to call them brothers [and sisters]' (2.11). The incarnation was integral to the Son's mission as sanctifier: 'since the children shared blood and flesh, likewise he also shared the same things, in order that by death he might nullify the one having the power of death' (2.14). This fellowship of flesh and blood is here associated with the believers' status as children. The familial bond is mentioned a third time in the same context: 'he was obligated to be like his brothers [and sisters] in all things, so that he might be a merciful and faithful high priest with respect to the things of God, for the purpose of atoning for the sins of the people' (2.17). Jesus' intimate identification with humanity is essential to his ministry as high priest. Based on the nature of Christ's high priestly work, the status of believers is eternal, 'for by one sacrifice he has perfected forever (εἰς τὸ διηνεκὲς) those being sanctified' (10.14).

55. Scholer, *Proleptic Priests*, p. 207.

Employment of kinship language to describe the relationship between Jesus and believers suggests that, through the incarnation, the exaltation of the Son above believers has been modified without erasing Jesus' superior status. Further confirmation for that suggestion is present in the declaration: 'we have become partners of Christ, if indeed the beginning of the conviction we hold fast confidently to the end' (3.14). While acknowledging Jesus' unique status as sanctifier and high priest, the author was concerned to demonstrate that Christ was not remote or distant from other members of the implied society; believers are siblings of and partners with the Son.

Leadership in the Implied Society. Having identified two related strata in the implied society (the Son and Believers), the possibility of further subdivision must be addressed. In the final chapter of Hebrews, the author mentioned 'leaders' (ἡγούμενοι; 13.7, 17, 24). Though this designation could be construed as indicative of refinement in the internal structure of the implied society, the specific statements do not support the conclusion that the leaders occupied an elevated stratum.

In the first mention of the leaders they are described as those 'who spoke the word of God to you' (13.7). A common conclusion is that the individuals identified in Heb. 13.7 were former leaders of the community who had died,[56] though their identification as the witnesses mentioned in Heb. 2.3 is uncertain.[57] Commenting on the position of these 'leaders', Attridge stated that 'they are unlikely to have been monarchical bishops, and some sort of presbyterial group is probably involved.'[58] With less reticence, James Moffatt identified the 'leaders' as 'primitive apostles and prophets'.[59] Both of these assertions exceed the direct evidence present in the epistle.

Designations such as elder/presbyter, apostle, and prophet are conspicuously absent from Hebrews. In the discussion of the grid of first-century Judaism, the numerous hierarchical titles employed in the

56. Attridge, *Hebrews*, p. 391; Bruce, *Hebrews*, p. 374; Ellingworth, *Hebrews*, p. 702; Lane, *Hebrews 9–13*, p. 526; Moffatt, *Hebrews*, p. 230.

57. Attridge, *Hebrews*, p. 391 accepts this possibility; Ellingworth, *Hebrews*, p. 702 concludes that 'there is no clear evidence that these leaders were the founders of the community'.

58. Attridge, *Hebrews*, p. 391.

59. Moffatt, *Hebrews*, p. 230.

synagogue were mentioned.[60] Within early Christianity a similar breadth of titles can be identified; the Pauline corpus contains nine such terms: ἀπόστολος, 'apostle', διάκονος, 'deacon', διδάσκολος, 'teacher', ἐπίσκοπος, 'overseer/bishop', εὐαγγελιστής, 'evangelist', κῆρυξ, 'preacher', ποιμήν, 'shepherd/pastor', πρεσβύτερος, 'elder', προφήτης, 'prophet'. The association of Hebrews with Pauline Christianity is ancient[61] and the relationship between the author and hellenistic Judaism is accepted widely.[62] Despite having connections to both communities, the author refrained from employing any hierarchical title to describe a human member of the implied society.

Selected words with titular associations were employed by the author, but never as a congregational title. προφήτης ('prophet') is employed twice (1.1; 11.32) to refer to the prophets of the former covenant. πρεσβύτερος ('elder') occurs once (11.2) as a designation applied to the patriarchs and other examples of faith under the former covenant. In Heb. 5.12 the believers are chided with the comment, 'though you should be teachers...again you need someone to teach you'. This use of διδάσκολος ('teacher') is functional rather than titular, indicating a task which all believers should be prepared to undertake.[63] Of the two remaining occurrences of potentially hierarchical language, one is metaphorical (ποιμήν ['shepherd/pastor'], 13.20), the other is a title (ἀπόστολος ['apostle'], 3.1), and both are applied to Jesus. Based on the frequency of occurrence of these community titles in the Pauline corpus, between six and fifteen occurrences should be expected in Hebrews.[64] The absence of such terminology to refer to anyone other

60. Cf. Lee I. Levine, 'Synagogue Officials: The Evidence from Caesarea and its Implications for Palestine and the Diaspora', in Avner Raban and Kenneth G. Holum (eds.), *Caesarea Maritima: A Retrospective after Two Millennia* (Leiden: E.J. Brill, 1996), pp. 392-400; Louis H. Feldman, *Studies in Hellenistic Judaism* (AGJU; Leiden: E.J. Brill, 1996), pp. 587-96; Leon, *The Jews of Ancient Rome*, pp. 167-94.

61. Eusebius, *Ecclesiastical History* 6.25.13-14.

62. Cf. Attridge, *Hebrews*, p. 5; Buchanan, *To the Hebrews*, p. 263; Lane, *Hebrews 1–8*, p. xlix.

63. Attridge, *Hebrews*, p. 158; Ellingworth, *Hebrews*, p. 302; James D.G. Dunn, *Unity and Diversity in the New Testament: An Inquiry into the Character of Earliest Christianity* (London: SCM Press; Valley Forge, PA: Trinity Press International, 2nd edn, 1990), p. 119.

64. In the seven generally accepted Pauline epistles, the indicated terms occur as titles 33 times in 28,189 words, for a frequency of 1.17/1000 words. In the remain-

than the Son constitutes supporting evidence for the conclusion that the only significant differentiation within the implied society is between the sanctifier and the sanctified.

To describe the leaders of the church, the author of *1 Clement* employed the same term found in Hebrews: ἡγούμενοι (1.3; 37.2). Unlike the author of Hebrews, the author of *1 Clement* was not reluctant to employ hierarchical language. Among the ecclesiastical authorities mentioned in the later document are the ἀπόστολος (5.3; 42.1, 2; 44.1; 47.1, 4), the ἐπίσκοπος (42.4, 5 [bis]; 44.1, 4), the πρεσβύτερος (44.5; 47.6; 54.2; 57.1), and the διάκονος (42.4, 5 [bis]). Literary connections between Hebrews and *1 Clement*, reflected in the ancient hypothesis that a Roman bishop named Clement wrote Hebrews, enhance the significance of this contrast. Further contrasts between Hebrews and *1 Clement* are discussed in the final chapter of this study.

As in portions of the discussion of group status, an inference drawn from the absence of hierarchical titles in Hebrews is an argument from silence, though, again, the silence is conspicuous. In Heb. 2.3 the author described the transmission of the evangel to the community: 'how will we escape, having neglected so great a salvation, which having been first spoken by the Lord, was confirmed to us by those who heard [him].' The circumlocution, 'those who heard him', refers to a group that probably included apostles.[65] The author does not, however, identify the human witnesses as 'apostles', reserving that title for the Son. To identify the 'leaders' as presbyters, apostles, or prophets, as did Attridge and Moffatt, is to tread on ground skirted by the author.[66]

Lane's evaluation of the status of the 'leaders' is consistent with the

ing six epistles of the Pauline corpus the titles occur 26 times in 9,630 words, for a frequency of 2.70/1000 words. Using these frequencies, the 5,675 words of Hebrews should contain between 6.64 and 15.32 occurrences of these terms as titles for members of the community.

65. Attridge (*Hebrews*, p. 67) commented on the similarity of Heb. 2.3 to 'the references in the later strata of early Christian literature to the apostolic tradition and its authenticity. Despite the similarities, there are significant differences. Hebrews is not searching for an authoritative apostolic foundation for a tradition. Yet neither is it polemicizing against such an 'early catholic' appeal to apostolic tradition.'

66. The failure to designate believers as 'priests', despite ascribing to them priestly status (Scholer, *Proleptic Priests*, pp. 10, 207), can be counted as another conspicuous silence with respect to hierarchical language. Believers are designated as priests in 1 Pet. 2.5, 9; Rev. 1.5; 5.10; 20.6.

evidence present in Hebrews. 'They may be characterized as charismat-
ically endowed leaders, whose authority derived exclusively from the
word they proclaimed and whose precedence was enhanced by preach-
ing alone... No other grounding and safeguarding of the position of the
leaders is provided than the authority that results from the word proclaimed.'[67] This limited authority is evident in the second mention of
the (presumably current) 'leaders': 'Obey your leaders and submit, for
they are keeping watch over your souls as ones giving account, in order
that they might do this with joy and not groaning; for this would be
harmful to you' (13.17). Accountability is a characteristic of a strong
grid society,[68] but the members of the implied society are not accountable directly to the 'leaders', rather the 'leaders' are accountable to
God.[69] The concluding phrase of Heb. 13.17 ('for this would be harmful
to you') can be associated with Heb. 4.13 ('no creature is hidden before
him, but all are naked and exposed to his eyes, before whom is our
account'), indicating that ultimately, like the 'leaders', all community
members are accountable to God.

The character of the relationship between the congregation and the
'leaders' can be inferred from the imperatives employed by the author
in Heb. 13.17. 'Obey' (πείθεσθε) describes a response 'not primarily
derived from a respect for constituted structures of authority. It is rather
the obedience that is won through persuasive conversation and that
follows from it.'[70] 'Submit' (ὑπείκετε) is a *hapax legomenon* in the
New Testament, though extra-biblical usage includes connotations of
personal respect: 'give one the first word, allow him to speak first'.[71]
Subordination to a hierarchical superior is not emphasized in these
directions to the congregation.

No further significant data on the authority of the 'leaders' are available. The third occurrence of ἡγούμενοι is in the closing greeting of the
epistle: 'Greet all your leaders and all the saints' (13.24). Although
Buchanan was reluctant to identify all members of the believing community as recipients of this greeting, Attridge is probably correct in

67. Lane, *Hebrews 1–9*, p. 526; Dunn, *Unity and Diversity*, p. 119.

68. Gross and Rayner, *Measuring Culture*, pp. 81-82.

69. Bruce, *Hebrews*, p. 385; Ellingworth, *Hebrews*, p. 723; Lane, *Hebrews 9–
13*, p. 555; Ellingworth and Nida, *The Letter to the Hebrews*, p. 333.

70. Lane, *Hebrews 9–13*, p. 554.

71. *LSJ*, p. 1855.

concluding that 'leaders and…saints' is 'simply a comprehensive way of referring to the whole community.'[72]

Mere recognition of individuals as leaders is not evidence of strong grid. A society may be described as strong grid only when:

1.   leadership positions are limited to an exclusive group within the society
2.   roles in the society exhibit strong asymmetry
3.   assignment of leadership roles is based on ascription rather than achievement, and
4.   members are accountable to the leaders.[73]

Based on the subdued manner in which the author introduced and described the 'leaders', their presence in the community does not constitute evidence that the implied society is strong grid.

In the discussion of the relationship between Christ and believers, no differentiation between clergy and laity is evident. All believers are among οἱ ἁγιαζόμενοι (the 'sanctified' or 'set apart'), all are partners of Christ, and all possess priestly status. Dunn commented:

> The clearest witness to this *resistance to institutionalization* is the Fourth Gospel and the Johannine epistles; but we can also detect signs of it in Hebrews and Revelation.

> To be sure there are 'leaders' active in the Hebrews' church (13.7, 17, 24), but they are defined more in terms of pastoral function than of office (13.17)…responsibility for service and exhortation is laid on the whole membership (6.10; 10.25; 12.15). Here too are distinct parallels with the charismatic community of Paul.

> The most striking feature of Hebrews at this point however is the way in which *ministry focuses in Christ in a complete and final manner*. He alone is called 'apostle' (3.1). He completes the fragmentary revelation given through the prophets of old (1.1f.). Above all, he is priest, high priest, priest according to the order of Melchizedek (2.7; 3.1; 4.14f. 5.1; etc.). His priesthood is so complete and exalted, his priestly ministry so perfect and final, that *there is no role or room left for any priestly intermediary within the Christian community*. A distinct priesthood belonged only to the past, to the era of shadow…*each believer can 'draw near' the presence of God for himself without depending on other believers or any human intermediary* (emphasis original).[74]

72.   Buchanan, *To the Hebrews*, p. 242; Attridge, *Hebrews*, p. 409.
73.   Gross and Rayner, *Measuring Culture*, pp. 79-82.

The leaders serve from the midst of the sanctified, priestly congregation, consistent with a weak grid structure, they do not govern the congregation.

Stratification of the Implied Society. Based on the implicit description
of the ideal society by the author of Hebrews, discussed above, the
structure of that society may be depicted as in table 6. The simplicity of
this structure, exhibiting little differentiation among the congregation,
suggests immediately that the implied society is a weak grid society.
Confirmation of this conclusion must await a comparison of the implied
society with first-century CE Judaism.

Table 6. *Stratification of the implied society according to the author of Hebrews*

Jesus Christ, Son of God	seated at the right hand of God; eternal high priest; the sanctifier; brother to believers
Congregation (Leaders and Believers)	the sanctified; partners of Christ; priests, all (including leaders) accountable to God

Transcendence of the First-Century Jewish Grid in the Implied Society

The levitical priesthood constituted an ancestral nobility in first-century
CE Judaism, and this nobility possessed certain exclusive prerogatives,
including access to the central sanctuary of the temple and consumption
of portions of the sacrificial offerings. In Hebrews the exclusive noble
status of the levitical priesthood is overturned. Defining the priesthood
of Jesus, the author admitted: 'the one about whom these things were
said belonged to another tribe, from which no one served at the altar;
for it is obvious that our Lord arose from Judah, concerning which tribe
Moses never spoke about priests' (7.13-14). Despite this irreparable
failing (from a Jewish perspective), Jesus rose to the highest possible
status, attaining the rank of high priest.

Further contrast with the first-century Jewish grid is evident in the
reference to the Christian altar: 'We have an altar from which those

74. Dunn, *Unity and Diversity*, pp. 118, 119-20.

serving in the tabernacle do not have authority to eat' (13.10). Though the interpretation of this statement has occasioned considerable dispute,[75] and discussion of the possibility that the 'altar' is a eucharistic meal must be deferred until the next chapter, the cultic exclusion of the levitical priesthood is clear. Those granted exclusive cultic privileges according to the Jewish grid are denied cultic privileges according to the grid of the implied society.

Jesus' entry into the true Holy of Holies, coupled with the invitation to all believers to follow him into this innermost sanctum, represents another challenge to the first-century Jewish grid. Priestly status has been granted to all members of the implied society, and all are welcomed into the divine sanctuary, challenging further the noble status of the levitical priesthood.

Lack of differentiation within the implied society, particularly when contrasted with the complex stratification of first-century Jewish society (table 4), suggests the conclusion that the implied society should be viewed as weak grid. The author's explicit challenges to the higher strata of Jewish society, with a non-levitical high priest, a non-levitical priesthood, and the cultic exclusion of the levitical priesthood, support this conclusion.

In the affirmation of past responses to persecution, the author provided further evidence that he envisioned the community of believers as a weak grid society.

> Remember the former days, after you were enlightened you endured a great struggle of suffering, sometimes being held up to derision with insults and affliction, sometimes becoming partners with those thus treated. For you also suffered together with the prisoners and you accepted with joy the plundering of your possessions, because you know that you have better, abiding possessions (10.32-34).

Joyful acceptance of the plunder is, in itself, evidence of weak grid. Douglas identified the 'affirmation of [the] value of material things' as a strong grid characteristic and associated 'affirmation of spiritual joys—asceticism' with weak grid.[76] Though short of asceticism, the author's afirmation of the community's joyful response to being victims of plunder is indicative of a weak grid society. A further non-materialistic tendency is evident in the paraenetic section of the letter:

---

75. Cf. Ellingworth, *Hebrews*, pp. 708-12; Lane, *Hebrews 9–13*, pp. 537-39.
76. Douglas, *Natural Symbols*, p. 143.

'the manner [of life] is not to be a lover of money, being satisfied with what one has' (13.5).

Viewing the response to persecution from an honor-shame perspective suggests the same conclusion. In the final paragraph of his essay on honor and social status, Julian Pitt-Rivers stated:

> The conceptual systems which relate to honour provide, when each is taken in its totality and in its varied contexts, a mechanism which distributes power and determines who shall fill the roles of command and dictate the ideal image which people hold of their society. At the ultimate level of analysis, honour is the clearing-house for the conflicts in the social structure, the conciliatory nexus between the sacred and the secular, between the individual and society and between systems of ideology and systems of action.[77]

The mechanism by which such systems of honor operate is the challenge-riposte. Honorable responses to a challenge include positive rejection (scorn, disdain, contempt) and counter-challenge.[78]

By accepting 'with joy' the challenge, the recipients violated the rules of challenge-riposte. Their (non)response should have resulted in dishonor,[79] yet they experienced joy and anticipation of 'better, abiding possessions'. With this reaction, they dismissed the validity of the prevailing concepts of honor and shame, 'pivotal values of the first-century mediterranean world',[80] both Jewish and gentile. Such a response violated conventional 'rules which relate[d] one person to others',[81] thereby reflecting the weak grid of the implied society.

Imprisonment was another category of dishonor in the Greco-Roman world.[82] By praising the believers for 'sometimes becoming partners with those thus treated' and 'suffer[ing] together with the prisoners' (10.33-34), again the author violated the rules of honor. Reiterating this rejection of customary perceptions of honor, the author exhorted the

77. Julian Pitt-Rivers, 'Honour and Social Status', in J.G. Peristiany (ed.), *Honour and Shame: The Values of Mediterranean Society* (Chicago: University of Chicago Press, 1966), pp. 19-77 (73).

78. Malina, *The New Testament World*, p. 36.

79. Malina, *The New Testament World*, p. 36.

80. Malina, *The New Testament World*, p. 28.

81. Douglas, *Natural Symbols*, p. viii.

82. Brian Rapske, *The Book of Acts in its First Century Setting*. III. *Paul in Roman Custody* (Grand Rapids: Eerdmans; Carlisle, UK: The Paternoster Press, 1994), pp. 288-98.

believers to 'remember the prisoners as having been imprisoned with them, the ill-treated as being with them in body' (13.3).

Explicit rejection of conventional standards of honor occurs in Hebrews. Jesus 'despised/disregarded the shame' of the cross (12.2), and in faithful response believers are exhorted to 'bear the disgrace he [Jesus] endured' (13.13). In terms of the prevailing view of honor, the implied society was weak grid.[83]

Locating the Implied Society According to Group and Grid

Examination of the data in Hebrews leads to the conclusion that the implied society is weak group and weak grid. These designations are not absolute measurements, but comparative evaluations. While possessing a clear group identity and a sense of continuity with the people of God under the former covenant, the implied society was distinct from first-century CE hellenistic Judaism. The weak group status of the implied society is evident in the boundary imagery employed by the author (in Hebrews boundaries are to be crossed, not avoided or defended), the exhortation to φιλοξενία ('hospitality'), and the lack of nationalistic or 'insider versus outsider' language. Weak grid is evident in the simplicity of the structure of the implied society (particularly when compared to the structure of first-century Judaism), the kinship between the Son and believers, the absence of evidence for an elevated leadership status, the tendency to minimize the importance of material posessions, and the explicit violation of the first-century Jewish grid (including the denial of levitical nobility and the rejection of the conventional standards of honor).

Confirmation for three points noted above (lack of nationalistic or 'insider versus outsider' language and absence of evidence for an elevated leadership status) depends on arguments from silence. As those points were addressed in the development of the argument the conspicuous nature of the silences was noted. One further defense for such

---

83. Cf. deSilva, *Despising Shame*, pp. 4, 296. After examining this example and other examples of the repudiation of the prevailing standards of honor and shame, deSilva concluded that the exhortation 'to disregard the estimation of honor by society in favor of preserving or enhancing honor in God's sight (as defined by the community's tradition and prophetic innovations within that tradition)' is a significant component of the message of Hebrews. Cf. *idem*, 'Despising Shame,' p. 459.

arguments from silence is possible. In the analysis of a weak group, weak grid society, an investigator is, to some extent, attempting to prove a negative: the society under investigation possesses neither strong group nor strong grid characteristics. Proving a negative is notoriously difficult, making arguments from silence perhaps inevitable.

Chapter 4

THE CRITIQUE OF THE LEVITICAL SYSTEM AND THE COSMOLOGY
OF THE AUTHOR'S IMPLIED SOCIETY

In their review of Douglas's work Isenberg and Owen commented that 'the most interesting aspect of Douglas' model for the religionist is its ability to correlate particular social organizations with cosmological structures.'[1] Having argued that the implied society depicted by the author of Hebrews is weak group, weak grid, the next task is to identify the cosmology implicit in the epistle and to assess that cosmology in terms of its coherence with the paradigmatic weak group, weak grid cosmology (table 2).

The focus of the present examination is on the author's critique of the levitical system; therefore, the aspects of cosmology relevant to that critique (the concept of sin and the attitude toward ritual) are addressed first. Following that analysis, other elements of the implicit cosmology are examined. Having determined the implicit cosmology of Hebrews, the coherence of that cosmology is assessed.

The Critique of the Levitical System

A major aspect of the sacrificial cult defined in Leviticus is the necessity to remedy the effects of sin (sin being understood in terms of cultic purity), thus restoring the relationship between God and his people.[2] The examination of the author's critique of that levitical

1.   Isenberg and Owen, 'Bodies, Natural and Contrived', p. 7.
2.   Gordon J. Wenham, *The Book of Leviticus* (NICOT; Grand Rapids: Eerdmans, 1979), pp. 16-29; John E. Hartley, *Leviticus* (WBC, Dallas, TX: Word Books, 1992), pp. lvi-lxxii; Baruch A. Levine, *Leviticus* (The JPS Torah Commentary; Philadelphia: Jewish Publication Society, 1989), pp. xxxvii-xxxix, 256-57; Jacob Milgrom, *Leviticus 1–16* (AB; Garden City, NY: Doubleday, 1991), pp. 49-51, 440-43.

system must address two issues: the concept of sin and the remedy for sin.

The Concept of Sin—External or Internal?
Four categories of sin concepts are described by the group/grid paradigm:

(A)   weak group, strong grid: failure; loss of face; stupidity
(B)   weak group, weak grid: a matter of ethics and interiority
(C)   strong group, strong grid: the violation of formal rules; focus on behavior instead of internal state of being
(D)   strong group, weak grid: a matter of pollution; evil lodged within person and society; sin much like a disease; internal state of being more important than adherence to formal rules, but the latter still valued.[3]

The major distinction is between sin viewed as the violation of formal, external regulations and sin viewed as an internal, ethical issue. By assessing the view of sin presented in Hebrews, determining whether sin is perceived primarily as an internal ethical problem or as an external legal violation, the first element in the cosmology of the implied society can be characterized.

References to Sin in Hebrews. The author of Hebrews employed ten nouns to refer to sin (ἀγνόημα, 'sins of ignorance', ἀδικία, 'wrongdoing', ἁμαρτία, 'sin', ἀνομία, 'lawlessness', ἀπείθεια, 'disobedience', ἀπιστία, 'unfaithfulness', παράβασις, 'transgression', παρακοή, 'disobedience', παραπικρασμός 'rebellion' and πειρασμός 'testing'—a total of 39 occurrences). Figure 2a shows the New Testament frequency of occurrence for ἁμαρτία and related words, figure 2b shows the frequency of occurrence for the other nouns used in Hebrews and their cognates, and figure 2c shows the frequency of occurrence for a broad spectrum of terms used to describe sin.[4] In all cases the frequency in

---

3.   Isenberg and Owen, 'Bodies, Natural and Contrived', pp. 7-8.
4.   All frequency plots in this study were generated with *Accordance* software, ver. 2.1. Data such as those depicted in figure 2 must be interpreted with caution. Some of the terms used to describe sin may have alternative usages not directly relevant to the issue of sin. One example is πειρασμός, which occurs in Jas 1.2 with the meaning 'testing' or 'trial', but the same word in Jas 1.12 carries connotations of 'temptation'. The impact of this problem on the above comments is minimal.

Hebrews exceeds the average frequency for the New Testament by a factor of more than 2.5.[5] The number of synonyms used by the author and the frequency of his usage suggests a significant concern with the problem of sin. That interest is evident in his declaration in the prologue that the Son 'made a purification for sins' prior to taking his seat at the right hand of God (1.3).

Sin as a violation of cultic purity is one category acknowledged by the author. Atonement for sins of ignorance (ἀγνόημα) committed by the people was a stimulus for the annual performance of the Yom Kippur sacrifices (9.7). Ironically, the remedy for sins of ignorance demonstrated the limitations of this view of sin and of the levitical remedy:

> the priests enter continually into the first tent performing their ministry, but into the second only the high priest once a year, not without blood which he offers for himself and for the people's sins of ignorance, the Holy Spirit demonstrating that the way into the sanctuary is not yet manifest while the first tent stands, which is a parable for the present time, during which are offered both gifts and sacrifices that are not able to perfect the conscience of the worshipper, only concerning foods and drinks and various washings, regulations of flesh until the time of setting right is imposed (9.6-10).

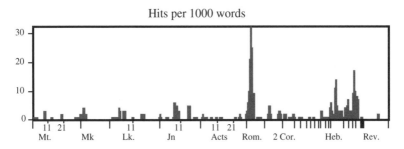

Hits per 1000 words

a. *Frequency of ἁμαρτάνω, ἁμάρτημα, and ἁμαρτία*

Occurrences in Hebrews of the terms noted refer specifically to sin in the context of that epistle. Removal of the other semantic domains from the frequency statistics would result in a decrease in occurrences outside of Hebrews, and a consequent increase in the concentration of sin terminology in Hebrews.

5.   Hebrews contains 5,675 words, 3.57% of the total words in the New Testament (159,056). Hebrews contains 12.27% of the total occurrences of ἁμαρτία and cognates, 13.22% of the total occurrences of the other terms and cognates employed in Hebrews, and 9.6% of the composite vocabulary for sin.

Hits per 1000 words

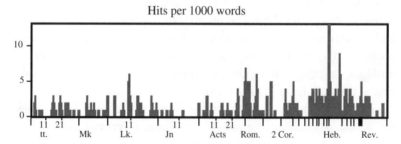

b. *Frequency of ἀγνόημα, ἀδικέω, ἀδίκημα, ἀδικία, ἀθετέω, ἀνομία,
ἀντιλογία, ἀπείθεια, ἀπειθέω, ἀπιστέω, ἀπιστία, ἐκπειράζω,
παραβαίνω, παράβασις, παραιτέομαι, παρακοὴ, παρακούω,
παραπικραίνω, παραπικρασμός, παραπίπτω, πειράζω, and πειρασμός*

Hits per 1000 words

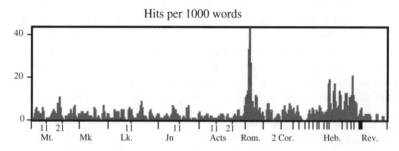

c. *Composite frequency of terms identified above and δελεάζω, ἐκκλίνω, ἐπαίρω,
παρανομέω, παρανομία, παράπτωμα, παρέρχομαι, προαμαρτάνω, πρόσκομμα,
προσκοπή, προσκόπτω, πταίω, ῥαδιούργημα, ῥαδιουργία, σκανδαλίζω,
σκάνδαλον, ὑπεραίρομαι, and ὑπερβαίνω.*

Figure 2. *New Testament frequency of occurrence of nouns and verbs
employed to refer to sin*

The description 'foods and drinks and various washings' is a clear
reference to Jewish purity laws.[6] By prefacing the mention of these
cultic purity regulations with the word μόνον ('only') and by stating that
the levitical sacrifices are restricted to 'the present time...until the time
of setting right is imposed,' the author argued for the inadequacy of the
external, forensic concept of sin and of the cultic remedy for sin. The
more serious problem is the perfection of the conscience.

6.　Attridge, *Hebrews*, pp. 242-43; Bruce, *Hebrews*, pp. 210-11; Ellingworth
and Nida, *The Letter to the Hebrews*, p. 188; Donald A. Hagner, *Hebrews* (NIBC;
Peabody, MA: Hendrickson; Carlisle, UK: Paternoster Press, 1995), p. 134.

Restating this point in his next paragraph, the author declared: 'For if the blood of goats and bulls and the sprinkled ashes of a heifer sanctifies those defiled with respect to the purity of the flesh, how much more the blood of Christ, who by an eternal spirit offered himself without blemish to God, will cleanse our conscience from dead works in order to serve the living God' (9.13-14). Again cultic purity is depicted as a lesser matter (remediable with lesser sacrifices) than the cleansing of the conscience.

In contrast with the ἀγνόημα ('sins of ignorance'), for which the cultus was an acceptable remedy, willful sin on the part of the believer could not be removed through levitical sacrifice (10.26; probably an allusion to Num. 15.30[7]). With this declaration in the fourth warning passage the author reiterated his concern with sin as a problem of the will, an internal problem. The external standard is not forgotten, but a more serious offense has become the primary concern. 'Someone who rejects the law of Moses is killed without mercy on the testimony of two or three witnesses; how much worse a punishment do you suppose he will deserve who tramples on the Son of God, and considers the blood of the covenant, with which he was sanctified, to be profane, and insults the spirit of grace?' (10.28-29). Employing a קל וחומר (*a fortiori*) argument, the author asserted the greater seriousness of the willful, internal sins of despising Christ, having contempt for Christ's sacrifice, and insulting the source of salvation.

The willful, internalized nature of sin is evident in the archetypal sin which the author discussed while advancing the argument begun in the second warning passage. A prominent motif in Hebrews is the wilderness wandering, and the sin committed by the generation that stood at Kadesh-barnea is described as rebellion (παραπικρασμός, παραπικραίνω; 3.8, 15, 16), testing (πειρασμός; 3.8), unbelief (ἀπιστία; 3.12, 19), and disobedience (ἀπειθέω, ἀπείθεια; 3.18; 4.6, 11). Two elements of the author's presentation demonstrate the internal nature of the sin about which the readers were being warned. First, the midrash on the psalm begins with the imperative, 'Watch out, brothers [and sisters], lest there be in some of you an evil heart of unbelief resulting in your stepping aside from the living God' (3.12). The locus of sin is the heart, whose thoughts and intentions are judged by the word of God (4.12). Second, the exhortation taken from the quotation of Ps. 95, 'Do not

7.   Lane, *Hebrews 9–13*, p. 292.

harden your hearts' (3.8; repeated in 3.15), is elaborated as 'exhort yourselves every day, while it is called "today," so that no one among you might be hardened by the deceitfulness of sin' (3.13). The symptoms of sin are related not to the violation of an external standard, but to internalized deception, unbelief, and hardening of the heart.

In harmony with the second and fourth warning passages, the third warning passage includes an emphasis on the internal problem. 'Solid food is for the mature, who because of the exercise of the senses have become trained in judging between good and evil' (5.14). Maturity is a matter not of adherence to a legal code, but of moral discernment. This warning passage includes one of the most severe evaluations of sin in the epistle: 'It is impossible…to renew again to repentance, while crucifying again for themselves the Son of God and exposing him to public ridicule' (6.4, 6). Though the language used to describe the perilous sin is metaphorical and the precise identification of the offense is subject to dispute, clearly the character of the sinful behavior is not formal violation of purity regulations, but willful rebellion against God.

Καρδία and συνείδησις in Hebrews. Two words that occur frequently in the discussion of sin in Hebrews are καρδία ('heart') and συνείδησις ('conscience').[8] The heart is described as being hardened and rebellious (3.8, 15; 4.7), deceived (3.10), evil and unbelieving (3.12), and judged by the word of God (4.12). Conversely the heart is the medium upon which the new covenant was to be inscribed (8.10; 10.16) and the heart could be strengthened by grace (13.9). The conscience is unaffected by the cultus (9.9; cf. 10.2), but is purified from dead works by the blood of Christ and is, therefore, able to worship the living God (9.14). A clear conscience is evidenced by a desire to behave honorably (13.18). The author may not have distinguished greatly between heart and conscience, for he urged his readers to 'approach with true hearts in full assurance of faith, hearts having been sprinkled from an evil conscience' (10.22).[9]

Surveys of the first-century CE understanding of καρδία and συνείδησις as theological/anthropological/ethical terms (i.e. ignoring

---

8.	The related term ψυχή occurs in Heb. 4.12; 6.19; 10.38, 39; 12.3; and 13.17, but in none of these instances is the relationship between sin and the ψυχή addressed.

9.	Similar correlations between καρδία and συνείδησις are present in Rom. 2.15 and 1 Tim. 1.5.

the anatomical usage of καρδία) demonstrate that these terms were associated with the internal nature of the person. Following the Septuagint and Pseudepigrapha, New Testament authors employed καρδία to refer to 'the centre of the inner life of man and the source or seat of all the forces and functions of soul and spirit.'[10] Usage of καρδία by the author of Hebrews (summarized in the paragraph above) conforms to this understanding, which Louw and Nida explained as 'the causative source of a person's psychological life in its various aspects, but with special emphasis upon thoughts.'[11]

Biblical Hebrew had no distinct word for 'conscience'; consequently, συνείδησις occurs only three times in the Septuagint and the related verb, σύνοιδα, occurs only twice. The Septuagint translators rendered ידע in Lev. 5.1 as σύνοιδεν, employing σύνοιδα as 'to know'. In Job 27.6 לבב was translated by σύνοιδα ἐμαυτῷ, conveying the Greek sense of moral conscience.[12] Both Eccl. 10.20 and the Codex Sinaiticus variant at Sir. 42.18 contain usages of συνείδησις as 'understanding', 'thought', or 'knowledge'.[13] Only in Wis. 17.10 was συνείδησις used in the moral sense common in hellenistic literature, where the conscience had the forensic function of prosecutor/judge.[14] In the first century CE Josephus employed συνείδησις as 'consciousness', 'knowledge of something', and 'mind', while Philo demonstrated familiarity with the forensic, hellenistic usage.[15]

New Testament occurrences of συνείδησις are dominated by the Pauline corpus (three occurrences in Romans, eight in 1 Cor., three in 2 Cor., six in the Pastoral Epistles; cf. two in Acts, five in Heb., three in 1 Pet.), leading to a suggestion that Paul introduced the term into the Christian vocabulary.[16] In a study of 1 Cor. 8 and 10, Paul Gooch

10. Friedrich Baumgärtel and Johannes Behm, 'καρδία', *TDNT*, III, p. 611. Philo was familiar with the significance of καρδία in the Septuagint, though he and Josephus preferred the term ψυχή as a designation for the center of the inner life; Baumgärtel and Behm, 'καρδία', pp. 610-11.

11. Louw and Nida, *Greek English Lexicon of the New Testament*, I, p. 321; §26.3.

12. Christian Maurer, 'σύνοιδα, συνείδησις', *TDNT*, VII, p. 909.

13. Maurer, 'σύνοιδα, συνείδησις', p. 909.

14. Maurer, 'σύνοιδα, συνείδησις', p. 909.

15. Maurer, 'σύνοιδα, συνείδησις', pp. 910-12.

16. Gerd Lüdemann, 'συνείδησις', in Horst Robert Balz and Gerhard Schneider (eds.), *Exegetical Dictionary of the New Testament*, I (trans. Virgil P. Howard, James W. Thompson, John W. Medendorp and Douglas W. Stott; 3 vols.; Grand

identified two senses in which Paul used συνείδησις: a 'minimal sense' of 'self-awareness', and a negative feeling based on past actions.[17] Considering the whole New Testament, Louw and Nida found a somewhat broader range of meaning for συνείδησις: 'the psychological faculty which can distinguish between right and wrong' and 'to be aware of information about something'.[18]

Malina cautioned against an imposition of individualistic, anachronistic notions of 'conscience' on the New Testament usage of συνείδησις:

> The Latin word *conscientia* and the Greek word *syneidesis* stand for 'with-knowledge', that is, knowledge with others, individualized common knowledge, commonly shared meaning, common sense. Conscience then refers to a person's sensitive awareness of one's public ego-image with the purpose of striving to align one's own personal behavior and self-assessment with that publicly perceived ego-image. A person with conscience is a respectable, reputable, and honorable person. Respectability, in this social context, would be the characteristic of a person who needs other people in order to grasp his or her own identity. *Conscience is a sort of internalization of what others say, do, and think about one, since these others play the role of witness and judge.* Their verdicts supply a person with grants of honor necessary for a meaningful, humane existence (emphasis mine).[19]

Even with this caveat, συνείδησις is understood in an internalized moral/ethical sense, not identical to an external, formal legal code.

The five usages of συνείδησις in Hebrews can be classified according to the categories identified above. In Heb. 9.9 and 9.14 συνείδησις has an internal, moral function, the latter instance contrasting συνείδησις with 'the purity of the flesh.' By assuming that the συνείδησις is susceptible to corruption by 'dead works' (9.14), the author associated the defiling of the conscience with immoral acts of which believers are expected to repent (6.1).[20] A close relationship between συνείδησις and καρδία is evident in Heb. 10.22 and the συνείδησις is described as being subject to the taint of 'evil', again indicating an internal, moral

Rapids, MI: Eerdmans, 1990), p. 301.

17. Paul W. Gooch, ' "Conscience" in 1 Corinthians 8 and 10', *NTS* 33 (1987), pp. 244-45, 252.

18. Louw and Nida, *Greek English Lexicon of the New Testament*, I, pp. 324, 335; §26.13; 28.4.

19. Malina, *The New Testament World*, pp. 63-64.

20. Cf. Attridge, *Hebrews*, p. 252; Bruce, *Hebrews*, p. 218.

understanding of συνείδησις. An association of συνείδησις with honorable living, as described by Malina, is explicit in Heb. 13.18. Only in Heb. 10.2 is συνείδησις used in the sense of 'knowledge', 'awareness', 'consciousness'.[21]

This brief survey demonstrates that both καρδία and συνείδησις are employed in Hebrews to refer to the inner-person. Although subtle distinctions are possible, a rigid division between the two terms is probably unwarranted. Alexander Sand commented that 'καρδία refers...to the *inner person*, the seat of understanding, knowledge and will, and takes on as well the meaning *conscience* (emphasis original).'[22] Such a blurring of the boundary between καρδία and συνείδησις was noted above in reference to Heb. 10.22.

The Concept of Sin in Hebrews. The author of Hebrews was aware of the externalized understanding of sin, an understanding rooted in the levitical concept of cultic purity. Nowhere did he deny the legitimacy of this perspective; instead he argued emphatically that such sins were of distinctly secondary significance when compared to internalized, moral/ethical sin. By associating the more serious aspects of sin with the καρδία and συνείδησις, the author declared a greater concern with the internal problem of sin than with the external, formal violation of a legal purity code.

Turning to the four categories of sin defined by the group/grid paradigm, the two strong grid alternatives can be rejected. Because of a complete lack of supporting evidence, case A (weak group, strong grid) is dismissed. The explicit priority of an inner state of being over formal rules eliminates case C (strong group, strong grid).

Deciding between the remaining alternatives is less straightforward. In the strong group, weak grid case (D), the 'internal state of being is more important than adherence to formal rules, but the latter [are] still valued.'[23] Here a question arises: the author acknowledged the category of 'sin as a violation of formal rules,' but did he 'value' that category? While he did not denigrate the 'regulations of flesh' (9.10), the author's

21. These conclusions are similar to those reached by Gary S. Selby, 'The Meaning and Function of Συνείδησις in Hebrews 9 and 10', *ResQ* 28 (1986), pp. 145-54 (148).

22. Alexander Sand, 'καρδία', in Balz and Schneider (eds.), *Exegetical Dictionary of the New Testament*, II, pp. 249-51 (250).

23. Isenberg and Owen, 'Bodies, Natural and Contrived', p. 8.

attitude can be characterized as dismissive, suggesting a negative answer to the question.

A second characteristic of the strong group, weak grid view is that 'sin is a matter of pollution; evil [is] lodged within person and society.'[24] According to the author, sin requires purification or cleansing (1.3; 9.14; 10.22), implying a view of sin as pollution, and both the heart and conscience can be contaminated by evil (3.12; 10.22). Rather than identifying such language as indicative of a strong group, weak grid cosmology, plausible alternative explanations can be offered. Language referring to the purification or cleansing of sin can be explained as a reflection of the original Jewish context from which the author and recipients had emerged to form the new covenant community. Such language offers valuable metaphors to describe the process of removal of sin without necessarily confirming all possible extensions of the metaphors. Addressing the second aspect, although an evil heart/ conscience can be understood as 'evil lodged within', the expressions in Hebrews are far short of Paul's lament: 'Now if I do what I do not want to do, I agree that the Law is good. But now no longer am I doing it, but the sin dwelling in me... And if I do what I do not want to do, no longer am I doing it, but the sin dwelling in me' (Rom. 7.16-17, 20). Viewed in contrast with these comments, the author's perspective can be distinguished from a strict strong group, weak grid view.

Finally, the weak group, weak grid (B) view of sin as 'a matter of ethics and interiority'[25] is fully consistent with the author's statements. With the overwhelming emphasis in Hebrews on sin as a matter of heart and conscience, the fundamental problem of sin is perceived as an interior, ethical matter. This analysis leads to the conclusion that the author's view of sin is most consistent with the weak group, weak grid cosmology. In the further examination of the cosmology of the implied society, this conclusion must be tested, particularly with respect to the possible overlap with the strong group, weak grid cosmology.

The Remedy for Sin—Ritualistic or Non-ritualistic?
Ritual has been defined as 'conscious and voluntary, repetitious and stylized symbolic bodily actions that are centered on cosmic structures

24. Isenberg and Owen, 'Bodies, Natural and Contrived', p. 8.
25. Isenberg and Owen, 'Bodies, Natural and Contrived', p. 8.
26. Evan M. Zuesse, 'Ritual', in Mircea Eliade (ed.), *The Encyclopedia of Religion*, pp. 405-22 (405).

and/or sacred presences.'[26] Contrasting explicitly the character of Christ's sacrifice with the character of the sacrifices offered by the levitical high priest, the author of Hebrews declared: 'For Christ did not enter into the handmade sanctuary, which is a copy of the true one, but into heaven itself, now appearing in the presence of God for us; nor in order to offer himself many times, as the high priest enters the sanctuary every year with the blood of another, since he would be required to suffer many times from the foundation of the world; but now he has appeared once at the consummation of the ages for the putting away of sin by his sacrifice' (9.24-26). Similarly, 'every priest stands daily ministering again the same sacrifices many times, which are never able to remove sins, but this one, having offered one sacrifice for sins, forever sat down at the right [hand] of God' (10.11-12). With references to sanctuaries, to the presence of God, and to repetitive actions, the author revealed a concern with ritual.

A major point of contrast in these declarations is reflected in the author's emphases on the multiplicity of the levitical sacrifices, the inefficacy of those levitical sacrifices, and the perfect nature of Christ's single, eternally effective sacrifice. These emphatic contrasts are evident in the concentration in Hebrews of language describing extremes of frequency ('once', 'once for all', 'many times', 'always', 'never') and duration ('forever', 'for all time') (figure 3).

The issues raised by the author are relevant to a group/grid examination of the cosmology of the implied society. Isenberg and Owen described the four paradigmatic attitudes to ritual as:

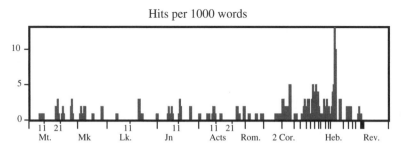

a. *Frequency of occurrence for ἀεί, ἅπαξ, ἑκάστοτε, ἐφάπαξ, μηδέποτε, οὐδέποτε, πάντοτε, πολλάκις, πολυμερῶς, πυκνός, and διὰ παντὸς*

Hits per 1000 words

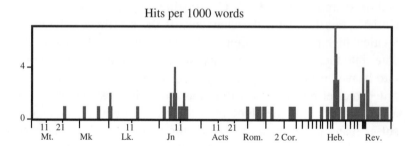

b. *Frequency of occurrence for εἰς (τὸν) αἰῶνα, εἰς (πάντας) τοὺς αἰῶνας, εἰς ἡμέραν αἰῶνος, εἰς τὸ διηνεκὲς, and εἰς τὸ παντελὲς*

Hits per 1000 words

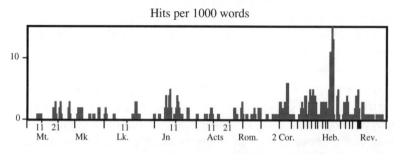

c. *Composite for the terms of frequency and duration identified above*

Figure 3. *New Testament frequency of occurrence of terms for extremes of frequency and duration*

(A)   weak group, strong grid: will be used for private ends if present; ego remains superior; condensed symbols do not delimit reality

(B)   weak group, weak grid: rejected; anti-ritual; effervescent; spontaneity valued

(C)   strong group, strong grid: a ritualistic society; ritual expresses the internal classification system

(D)   strong group, weak grid: ritualistic; ritual focused upon group boundaries, concerned with expelling pollutants (witches) from social body[27]

By examining the author's contrast between the levitical rituals and the sacrifice of Christ, the second element of the cosmology of the implied society can be assessed.

27. Isenberg and Owen, 'Bodies, Natural and Contrived', pp. 7-8.

Inefficacy of the Levitical Cultus. The author presented a consistent, multifaceted argument that the cultus was, ultimately, an inadequate remedy for sin. He introduced the point with a rhetorical question: 'If, therefore, there was perfection through the levitical priesthood, for the people had received legislation concerning it, why was there still a need for another priesthood to be raised up, according to the order of Melchizedek, and not called "according to the order of Aaron"?' (7.11). The clearly implied answer is that perfection was not available through the levitical priesthood.

At the climax of the cultic discussion in Hebrews the limitations of the cultus are described in explicit terms. Another rhetorical question raises the issue: 'For the law, possessing a shadow of the good things to come, not the true form of those things, can never perfect those approaching every year with the same sacrifices that they offer continually; otherwise would they not have ceased being offered, because those serving, once cleansed, would never again have a consciousness of sins?' (10.1-2). Answering his own question, the author declared that the cultus had, in fact, the opposite result, 'but in them [the sacrifices] is a remembrance of sins every year' (10.3). He then annnounced his evaluation of the cultus: 'for it is impossible for the blood of bulls and goats to take away sins' (10.4). After a brief midrash on Ps. 40, describing the work of 'the one who came into the world' (10.5), the author pronounced the verdict on the cultus: 'he abolished the first in order that he might establish the second' (10.9). Ellingworth described this comment as 'the strongest negative statement the author has made or will make about the OT cultus.'[28]

Not content merely to pronounce this verdict, the author persisted in his criticism of the levitical system. The repeated sacrifices of the cultus are 'never able to remove sins' (10.11). This declaration reiterates a point made earlier: the ministrations of the levitical cultus are 'not able to perfect the conscience of the worshipper' (9.9), 'the law...can never perfect those approaching every year with the same sacrifices that they offer continually' (10.1). Reflecting on such absolute statements Theodore Stylianopoulos commented 'that the inadequacy of the Mosaic cult is stated in rather sharp terms. The whole intent of the passage [Heb. 10.1-18] is to establish a radical contrast between the inefficacy of the Mosaic sacrifices and the effectiveness of Christ's sacrifice.'[29]

---

28. Ellingworth, *Hebrews*, p. 504.
29. Theodore G. Stylianopoulos, 'Shadow and Reality: Reflections on Hebrews

The Perfect Work of Christ. As Stylianopoulos noted, the nullification of the levitical cultus is not the final word from the author of Hebrews, the goal is to establish the surpassing value of Christ's work. The transition was anticipated in the discussion of Christ's priesthood: 'for there was a nullification of the earlier commandment because of its weakness and inefficacy—for the law perfected nothing—and an introduction of a better hope through which we draw near to God' (7.18-19).

Two aspects of Christ's priestly ministry are highlighted: mediation and sacrifice. Christ 'is also able to save for all time those who approach God through him, living always to intercede for them' (7.25). This mediatorial function is mentioned again: 'he is the mediator of a new covenant' (9.15).

References to Christ's self sacrifice are more numerous than those to his mediation. In contrast with the multiplicity of levitical offerings, Christ 'once for all...offered himself' (7.27). Functioning as high priest, 'he entered once for all into the sanctuary, eternal redemption having been secured' (9.12). With that blood, he cleansed 'our conscience' (9.14). That self-sacrifice, bearing 'the sins of many', was the purpose for his advent 'at the consummation of the ages' (9.26, 28), and was a prelude to his exaltation (10.12). Believers are the beneficiaries of that sacrifice; 'we have been sanctified by the offering of the body of Jesus Christ once for all' (10.10), 'for by one sacrifice he has perfected forever those being sanctified' (10.14).

The Nonritualistic Nature of Christ's Work. Repetitive performance is part of the essence of ritual.[30] Such repetition is mentioned explicitly as a characteristic of the cultus. The sacrifices must be offered 'daily' (7.27), with the priests entering the sanctuary 'continually' (9.6), 'every year' (9.25). Innovation is not valued in ritual; 'ritualism is taken to be a concern that efficacious symbols be correctly manipulated and that the right words be pronounced in the right order.'[31] Consequently, innovation is not characteristic of the cultus; the ministrants approach the levitical altar 'every year with the same sacrifices that they offer continually' (10.1). Because the ritual must be performed continually and invariably, the work of the levitical priests is never complete; 'every priest stands daily ministering again the same sacrifices many times,

10:1-18', *Greek Orthodox Theological Review* 17 (1972), pp. 215-30 (223-24).
    30. Zuesse, 'Ritual', p. 406.
    31. Douglas, *Natural Symbols*, p. 9.

which are never able to remove sins' (10.11).

Christ's work, as presented by the author of Hebrews, is a perfect contrast to the ritualistic cultus. The effects of Christ's ministry are 'for all time' (7.25), 'eternal' (9.12, 15). Twice the author employed perfect tense verbs to describe the effect of Christ's sacrifice (10.10, 14). Repetition of the sacrifice of Christ is impossible because of the 'once for all' (7.27; 9.12; 10.10) nature of Christ's work.[32] The very nature of Christ's self-sacrifice is that of a single sacrifice (10.12, 14). Whereas the cultus was instituted for 'the present time' (9.9), Christ's climactic, eschatological work was performed 'once at the consummation of the ages for the putting away of sin by his sacrifice' (9.26), and his return will not include a repeat performance (9.28). While the levitical priests stood performing their never-complete tasks, Christ 'sat down at the right [hand] of God' (10.12). Lest anyone doubt the non-repeatable nature of Christ's sacrifice, the author concluded the cultic section of the epistle with the aphorism, 'where there is forgiveness of these things, there is no longer an offering for sin' (10.18).

Effervescence in the Community's Worship of God. Ritualism and effervescence, as described by Douglas, are polar opposites. While the former is characteristic of strong group, strong grid societies, the latter is evident where both group and grid are weak. In ritualistic societies 'ritual differentiation of roles and situations', attribution of 'magical efficacy…to symbolic acts (e.g. sin and sacraments)', and 'symbolic distinctions between inside and outside' are evident.[33] Conversely, in an effervescent society 'spontaneous expression' is preferred and no interest in 'ritual differentiation', 'magicality', or 'symbolic expressions of inside/outside' is evident.[34]

According to the author of Hebrews, the levitical cultus was unquestionably ritualistic. The annual cycle of sacrifices distinguished between priests and laity, between the high priest and other priests, between the outer precincts and the Holy of Holies, and between the Day of Atonement and all other days, demonstrating 'ritual differentiation of roles

---

32. These occurrences of ἐφάπαξ are three of the five New Testament occurrences of this word (the remaining occurrences are Rom. 6.10 and 1 Cor. 15.6). Similarly eight of the 14 New Testament occurrences of ἅπαξ are in Hebrews, and four of the eight are in the cultic section of the epistle.

33. Douglas, *Natural Symbols*, pp. 73-74.

34. Douglas, *Natural Symbols*, p. 74.

and situations'. Magic (the belief in the efficacy of symbolic actions[35]) can be inferred as a characteristic of the cultus; the author's multiple declarations that the cultus was ineffective imply that a devotee of the cultus would have asserted the contrary. To the author's claim that the sacrifices produced not a sense of forgiveness but of 'remembrance of sins every year' (10.3), Philo can be cited as a counterpoint: 'it would be foolish to have the sacrifices working remembrance instead of oblivion to sin.'[36] 'Symbolic distinctions between inside and outside' are present in the sacred architecture of the sanctuary.

The implied society can be characterized as effervescent. In Hebrews ritual differentiation and symbolic distinctions between inside and outside are countered by the boundary-crossing imagery employed in the epistle and the minimal internal structure of the community. Lacking any mention of repeated symbolic actions, the author provided no evidence of magicality. Worshipping believers are exhorted to 'offer up continually a sacrifice of praise to God, which is the fruit of lips confessing his name. Do not forget the doing of good or the fellowship; for with such sacrifices God is well pleased' (13.15-16).[37] In the implied society, the cultus has been replaced by praise, service, and active fellowship, activities more closely akin to 'spontaneous expression' than to ritual sacraments.

A probable reflection of the author's non-ritualistic tendencies is his treatment of the early Christian rituals of baptism and eucharist. With unambiguous New Testament references to each (baptism: Acts 8.36-38; 9.18; 10.47-48; 19.5; Rom. 6.4; 1 Cor. 1.14-17; eucharist: Lk. 22.19; 1 Cor. 11.17-34), the practice of these rituals in the earliest Christian communities is certain.[38] Despite this common practice, the

---

35. Douglas, *Natural Symbols*, p. 8.

36. Philo, *Spec. Leg.* 1.215. Elsewhere Philo conceded that if the sacrifices are offered without sincerity, 'it is not a remission but a reminder of past sins which they effect'; *Vit. Mos.* 2.107.

37. Attridge (*Hebrews*, pp. 399-401) noted that the phrase 'sacrifice of praise' could be interpreted as a literal, animal sacrifice, but that the author countered such an interpretation with the elaboration, 'which is the fruit of lips confessing his name'. The content of worship, according to Attridge, was 'primarily prayer rather than a ritual act'.

38. Oscar Cullman (*Early Christian Worship* [trans. A. Stewart Todd and James B. Torrance; SBT; Chicago: Henry Regnery Company, 1953], pp. 20, 25) included the eucharist in the 'basis of early Christian Worship' and found evidence of a

author referred to baptism only through a metaphor and he omitted mention of the eucharist.

In two contexts the author referred to entry into the community of believers as 'enlightenment' (6.4; 10.32). The earlier context added to enlightenment the phrases 'having become partners of the Holy Spirit and having tasted both the goodness of the word of God and the powers of the coming age' (6.4-5). To have placed these four images in apposition to one another without an explicit reference to baptism is noteworthy.[39]

The author's only allusion to baptism occurs in Heb. 10.22: 'let us approach with true hearts in full assurance of faith, hearts having been sprinkled from an evil conscience and *bodies having been washed with pure water*' (emphasis mine). Recent commentators are agreed that the washing is a reference to Christian baptism, particularly since the act is coupled with confession ('let us hold fast to the confession of hope without wavering, for the one who promised is faithful'; 10.23).[40]

Twice the author used the word βαπτισμός, but in neither case was Christian baptism the referent. In the former instance, βαπτισμός is plural and is one component of an elementary catechism, which consisted of 'repentance from dead works and faith in God, teaching of baptisms [βαπτισμῶν] and laying on of hands, and resurrection of the dead and eternal judgement' (6.1-2). The plural form is unusual in the New Testament, occurring only here, Heb. 9.10, and Mk 7.4. F.F. Bruce noted that none of the foundational items listed in Heb. 6.1-2 is distinctly Christian, 'practically every item could have its place in a fairly orthodox Jewish community. Each of them, indeed, acquires a new significance in a Christian context; but the impression we get is that existing Jewish beliefs and practices were used as a foundation on which to build Christian truth.'[41] Consequently, Bruce translated βαπτισμῶν as 'ablutions',[42] identifying the 'baptisms' as Jewish ritual washings. This conclusion is consistent with the other New Testament

'rudimentary liturgy' for baptism in 'the very earliest period'.

39. Ellingworth (*Hebrews*, p. 320) commented that 'the ritual aspect of baptism was not prominent in the author's mind'.

40. Attridge, *Hebrews*, pp. 288-89; Ellingworth, *Hebrews*, pp. 523-24; Lane, *Hebrews 9–13*, pp. 287-88.

41. Bruce, *Hebrews*, p. 139.

42. Bruce, *Hebrews*, p. 137.

occurrences of the plural form, both of which are unambiguous references to Jewish ritual practice.[43]

R. Williamson examined the alleged allusions to the eucharist in Hebrews and concluded that 'there is little or no evidence in Hebrews of involvement...in eucharistic faith and practice... Hebrews is silent at points where an explicit and unambiguous reference to the Eucharist might have been expected.'[44] The supposed allusions to the eucharist are tenuous:

1. 'blood and flesh' (2.14) as a reference to the individual elements: In the context of Hebrews the phrase is intended to emphasize Jesus' humanity.

2. tasting 'the heavenly gift' (6.4) as a description of eucharistic practice: The more likely interpretation is that this phrase is one of several employed to 'describe vividly the reality of the experience of personal salvation enjoyed by the Christians addressed.'[45] In the only occurrence of γεύομαι ('to taste') in Hebrews outside this immediate context (2.9), the usage is figurative, expressing 'experience' rather than literal consumption.

3. Jesus' entry into the sanctuary 'by his own blood' (9.12) as an allusion to the eucharistic cup: Williamson responded that 'the word [blood] there, as elsewhere in Hebrews, almost certainly refers to the death of Christ viewed as a sacrifice.'[46]

4. the substitution of τοῦτο for ἰδού ('this' for 'behold') in the quotation from the Septuagint (9.20; quoting Exod. 24.8) as a reflection of the words of institution spoken at the last supper: This assertion places undue emphasis on the alteration of one word and ignores other alterations in the same quotation (διέθετο to ἐνετείλατο ['he decreed' to 'he commanded']; κύριος πρὸς ὑμᾶς to πρὸς ὑμᾶς ὁ θεός ['Lord with you' to

43. DeSilva ('Hebrews in Social-Scientific Perspective', p. 3) interpreted the 'baptisms' of Heb. 6.2 as a Christian ritual, but did not suggest an explanation for the plural form. The cognate neuter form, βάπτισμα, never occurs in the New Testament as a plural.

44. R. Williamson, 'The Eucharist and the Epistle to the Hebrews', *NTS* 21 (1975), pp. 300-12 (309).

45. Lane, *Hebrews 1–8*, p. 141; cf. Williamson, 'The Eucharist and the Epistle to the Hebrews', p. 303; Attridge, *Hebrews*, p. 167.

46. Williamson, 'The Eucharist and the Epistle to the Hebrews', p. 305.

'God with you']; the second of which seems to argue against a eucharistic motive).[47]

5. 'the blood of Jesus' and 'his flesh' as an evocation of the last supper (10.19-20): As argued above, these phrases are more likely references to the death of the incarnate Jesus.

6. 'the altar' as the eucharistic table (13.10): Such an interpretation falters on several counts. The statement in Heb. 13.10 does not make the positive assertion that Christians have a right to eat from the 'altar'. The preceding sentence seems to argue against the soteriological benefit of 'foods'. No Christian text employs the word 'altar' as a reference to the eucharist until 'more than a century after the writing of Hebrews'.[48] The 'deliberate ambiguity' of Heb. 13.10 suggests that the author was referring 'to the sacrifice of Christ in all of the complexity with which that is understood in Hebrews'.[49]

If the author intended to allude to the eucharist, he avoided two opportunities to do so. In his equation of Melchizedek and Jesus, the author omitted any mention of the bread and wine brought to the patriarch by Melchizedek (Heb. 7.1-3; cf. Gen. 14.17-20). The interpretive possibilities of this element of the story are evident in Philo's allegorizing of the act and in Cyprian's discovery of a typological foreshadowing of the eucharist.[50] The second 'missed' opportunity was the lack of elaboration on the potential symbolism of the table and bread of presence in the Holy Place (9.2). Williamson's conclusion that the author 'did not share in the eucharistic faith and practice of other segments of

---

47. The dismissal of this alteration is not inconsistent with the earlier stress on the modification to the new covenant passage from Jeremiah. These two cases are not completely analogous because in the quotation of the Jeremiah text the author quoted the Septuagint faithfully (τῷ οἴκῳ Ἰσραήλ; 8:10 [Jer. 31.33; LXX 38.33]) and then altered the phrase when he repeated the quotation (πρὸς αὐτούς; 10.16).

48. Lane, *Hebrews 9–13*, p. 538.

49. Attridge, *Hebrews*, p. 396.

50. Philo, *Leg. All.* 3.79-82; Cyprian, *Epistles* 62.3-4 (some editors count this epistle as number 63). Less explicit eucharistic references to Melchizedek are present in Ambrose, *On the Mysteries* 45; and *idem*, *On the Christian Faith* 3.87-89. Both Cyprian and Ambrose reflect the influence of Hebrews in their treatments of Melchizedek. The author's silence on this point is a major obstacle to accepting Swetnam's ('Christology and the Eucharist', p. 94) conclusion that 'the eucharist emerges...as a central point of the epistle'.

the Early Church'[51] may be overstated, but his judgment that 'the sacrifice of Christ was of a kind that rendered obsolete every form of cultus that placed a material means of sacramental communion between God and the worshipper'[52] is consistent with the non-ritualistic leanings of the author of Hebrews in his critique of the levitical system.[53]

The Remedy for Sin in Hebrews. In his discussion of the passage from the old to the new in Hebrews, Jean-Paul Michaud described the new 'cult': 'It has no ritual: it is existential, it belongs to daily life and is distinguished by 'beneficence and mutual community aide': *eupoiia* and *koinonia*. Here, the word 'sacrifices' has changed meaning.'[54] Joseph Moingt employed more vivid language, finding in Hebrews a 'gospel rupture with ritual.'[55] Clearly, the remedy for sin described in Hebrews cannot be reconciled with the ritualistic strong group, strong grid cosmology; the author argued persistently and specifically against such a view of ritual in the implied society. For similar reasons, the other ritualistic quadrant (strong group, weak grid) is equally inconsistent

---

51. Williamson, 'The Eucharist and the Epistle to the Hebrews,' p. 311.

52. Williamson, 'The Eucharist and the Epistle to the Hebrews,' p. 310.

53. For analyses that conclude that the author was referring to the eucharist in a positive manner, see James Swetnam, 'On the Imagery and Significance of Hebrews 9,9-10', *CBQ* 28 (1966), pp. 155-73; *idem*, '"The Greater and More Perfect Tent". A Contribution to the Discussion of Hebrews 9,11', *Bib* 47 (1966), pp. 91-106; *idem*, 'Christology and the Eucharist'. Swetnam ('On the Imagery and Significance of Hebrews 9,9-10', p. 173) conceded that his interpretation has 'serious difficulties' and qualified his conclusions with such words and phrases as 'tentative' and 'it would not seem rash' ('The Greater and More Perfect Tent', pp. 105, 106). For another Roman Catholic treatment, reaching similar (though less reluctant) conclusions, see Barnabas Lindars, *The Theology of the Letter to the Hebrews* (NTT; Cambridge: Cambridge University Press, 1991), pp. 138-42.

54. Jean-Paul Michaud, 'Le passage de l'ancien au nouveau, selon l'épître aux Hébreux', *ScEs* 35 (1983), pp. 33-52 (44). 'Il n'a rien de rituel: il est existentiel, il appartient à la vie quotidienne et se définit par la "bienfaisance et l'entraide communautaire": *eupoiia* et *koinonia*. Ici, le mot "sacrifices" a changé de sens.'

55. Joseph Moingt, 'Prêtre "selon le nouveau testament": à propos d'un livre récent', *RSR* 69 (1981), pp. 573-98 (588). Moingt's complete sentence is: 'C'est par ce changement de sens du mot sacrifice (déjà connu des prophetes) que passe la rupture évangélique avec le rituel, par un appel à transformer les relations humaines et les conditions sociales et économiques d'existence.'

with this element of the cosmology of the implied society. In the latter case the failure by the author to mention the Yom Kippur scapegoat is extremely significant; such an image would have been ideal to describe the practice of 'expelling pollutants...from the social body.'[56]

Elimination of the weak group, strong grid cosmology from consideration is based on less explicit evidence. In this quadrant ritual (if present at all) is a private matter, but Hebrews offers no support for such a view of ritual. The author had little to say about individuals. Johnsson commented: 'The anthropology of Hebrews cannot be separated from its ecclesiology. The individual per se is never in view in the pamphlet: it is always man as a member of the cultic community with which we have to do.'[57] Believers are encouraged to participate in 'the gathering together of yourselves' (10.25). Ultimately, the goal of the pilgrimage of the faithful is expressed not in terms of private, individual salvation or reward, but in terms of membership in a city, a kingdom, 'the assembly of the firstborn who have been enrolled in heaven' (12.23). Superiority of the ego (a weak group, strong grid characteristic) is absent from Hebrews.

Christ's once-for-all self-sacrifice, solving the fundamental problem of sin, was an unrepeatable event by virtue of its singular nature and by virtue of the eternal effects of that sacrifice. As an unrepeatable sacrifice, Christ's death precludes the existence of active ritual practice in the implied society. Ritual is replaced with praise of God and service to fellow believers (13.15-16). The implied society reflects an attitude toward ritual most consistent with the weak group, weak grid cosmology.

Some recent examinations of the cultic section of Hebrews might seem to contradict this conclusion, but the contradiction is only apparent. Johnsson, who described the implied society as a 'cultic community', conceded: 'We have not been able to point to any liturgical acts...of the community.'[58] John Dunnill characterized the 'cultic elements in Hebrews' as 'integral to the work' and concluded that 'Hebrews claims for itself the image of a *liturgy*, a symbolic action in the sacred sphere: more particularly, a *covenant-renewal rite*, of which the book's words comprise a long prophetic exhortation' (emphasis

---

56. Isenberg and Owen, 'Bodies, Natural and Contrived', p. 7.
57. Johnsson, 'Defilement and Purgation in the Book of Hebrews', p. 432.
58. Johnsson, 'Defilement and Purgation in the Book of Hebrews', pp. 432, 445.

Going Outside the Camp

original).[59] Despite the ritualistic impression of Dunnill's conclusion, his elaboration on that conclusion resolves the issue in favor of a non-ritualistic view of worship in the implied society:

> What results is a liturgical understanding of the present moment, expressing a theology of the actual presence of God. If Christians have found here warrant for a Christian expiatory cultus and a Christian separative priesthood it has been in contravention of the argument—for it insists that 'there is no longer any offering for sin' (10.18) and that Christ alone is the priestly mediator—and equally in contravention of the pattern of symbolism taken as a whole. This has been illustrated by the book's vision of worship as face-to-face relationship between humanity and God expressed in a pattern of *speech-acts*—oaths, promises, blessings, curses, and praise—a whole economy of verbal exchange which is tacitly offered here in place of the subpersonal mediation of 'goats and calves', an interchange of gifts replacing the trade in blood, and which fills in the sense of what is really meant by the metaphor of 'drawing near to the throne of grace' (emphasis original).[60]

Johnsson and Dunnill were correct to emphasize the significance of the cultic language in Hebrews. Of the 28 New Testament occurrences of θυσία ('sacrifice'), 15 are in Hebrews. Of the nine occurrences of προσφορά ('offering'), five are in Hebrews. Frequency of occurrence for a broad spectrum of cultic terminology is depicted in figure 4. The concentration of cultic terminology in Hebrews is unquestionable.[61] This language does not demonstrate that the author was seeking to impose a new ritual on the community; rather, he was contrasting the new community with the old and was describing the work of Christ and the worship of believers with terms and metaphors relevant to the readers. A personal, 'face-to-face' relationship with God, as described by Dunnill, is completely consistent with the non-ritualistic, effervescent, spontaneous worship expected in a weak group, weak grid society.

59. Dunnill, *Covenant and Sacrifice in the Letter to the Hebrews*, pp. 239, 261.

60. Dunnill, *Covenant and Sacrifice in the Letter to the Hebrews*, pp. 261-62.

61. Hebrews contains 38 of the 146 occurrences of the indicated terms. With 26.0% of the total, the frequency in Hebrews is 7.3 times greater than would be expected in an even New Testament distribution of cultic language.

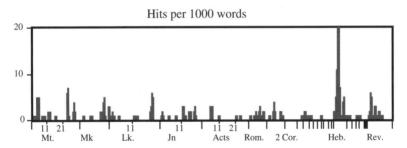

Figure 4. *New Testament frequency of occurrence for cultic terms
(ἀπαρχή, δῶρον, θυμίαμα, θυμιατήριον, θυσία, θυσιαστήριον, ἱλασμός,
ἱλαστήριον, ὁλοκαύτωμα, πάσχα, προσφορά, σφάγιον, ἄρτοι τῆς
προθέσεως/πρόθεσις τῶν ἄρτων, κιβωτὸς τῆς διαθηκῆς, and περὶ ἁμαρτίας)*

Scholer labeled the citizens in the implied society with the cultic term
'priests'. He included all believers in this category, and described
Christian activity as 'enjoying access to God and offering sacrifices of
praise, worship, and thanksgiving since the end days are here (e.g. 1.2;
9.26), and all the while they are anticipating the eschatological future
when full and direct access will be enjoyed.'[62] The believers' 'priestly
status is not found in their performance of any sort of atoning ritual
service, but solely in their uninhibited access to God, made possible by
the past and present priestly service rendered by Christ himself.'[63] Both
Scholer and Dunnill agreed that worship in the implied society consists
of direct, personal access to God, an access available to all members.
Such worship is the antithesis of 'a ritualistic society' where 'ritual expresses the internal classification system',[64] but is thoroughly consistent
with the cosmology of the paradigmatic weak group, weak grid society.

The Cosmology of the Implied Society

In the examination of the critique of the levitical system, two elements
of the cosmology of the implied society (sin and ritual) have been discussed at length. To complete the examination of the cosmology the
remaining components must be addressed. Because purity and magic
are related closely to sin and ritual, these four constituents are treated
together. Because data for an assessment of the attitude to trance are

62. Scholer, *Proleptic Priests*, p. 205.
63. Scholer, *Proleptic Priests*, p. 207.
64. Isenberg and Owen, 'Bodies, Natural and Contrived', p. 7.

absent from Hebrews,[65] that cosmological element is omitted in the following discussion. The remaining elements are treated individually.

Purity, Sin , Ritual, and Magic

The author's treatment of purity is analogous to his treatment of sin: purity as cultic sanctity is acknowledged, but is subordinated to a redefined concept of purity. Levitical purity issues (βαπτισμῶν διδαχῆς ['teaching of baptisms']) are included in the 'foundation' (6.2) that must be transcended, and are among the regulations to be surpassed in 'the time of setting right' (9.10). Restoration of levitical purity requires lesser sacrifices than those required to cleanse the conscience (9.13-14). While the earthly sanctuary can be cleansed with levitical sacrifices, better sacrifices are required for the heavenly sanctuary (9.23).[66] The levitical sacrifices are not sufficient to cleanse the interiorized impurity of which the worshipper remains conscious (10.2).

Purification of sins was an essential aspect of the Son's incarnational mission (1.3). Through his single, once-for-all sacrifice, believers have been sanctified permanently (2.11; 10.10, 14; 13.12). The effects of Christ's sacrifice cleansed the believers' hearts 'from dead works' (9.14) and 'from an evil conscience' (10.22). Holiness as a prerequisite to entering God's presence (a concept in harmony with levitical principles) is now parallel to 'peace with all' (12.14). Defilement is associated with 'bitterness' (12.15). Marital fidelity is a requirement for those who wish to remain 'undefiled' (13.4).[67]

As was the case with sin, external purity is recognized, but internal purity is emphasized; purity has been redefined as an internal, moral issue (related to the conscience and including peaceful relations with others and marital fidelity) rather than as an external, formal, forensic matter. The powerful strong group, strong grid concern for purity, with 'well-defined purification rituals' and where 'purity rules define and maintain social structure'[68] is absent from Hebrews. The 'strong con-

---

65. None of the New Testament terms associated with dreams or visions (ἔκστατις, ἐνυπνιάζομαι, ἐνύπνιον, ὄναρ, ὀπτασία, ὅραμα, ὅρασις) occurs in Hebrews.

66. Attridge ('The Uses of Antithesis in Hebrews 8–10', p. 8) has argued that in the antitheses of Heb. 8–10 the heavenly realm is associated with 'interior realities'.

67. According to Douglas ('Cultural Bias', pp. 224, 232) illicit sexuality as a form of pollution is common to all four quadrants;.

68. Isenberg and Owen, 'Bodies, Natural and Contrived', p. 7.

cern for purity' in the strong group, weak grid society[69] is likewise inconsistent with the cosmology of the implied society. Silence on the issues characteristic of weak group, strong grid societies renders a definitive conclusion impossible, though the tendency of the author appears to be more consistent with the anti-purity stance of the weak group, weak grid cosmology than with the 'pragmatic attitude' of the weak group, strong grid alternative.[70] Given this conclusion, the author's employment of purity language despite his anti-purity stance can be explained as a reaction against the society from which his community emerged (strong group, strong grid Judaism) and/or as a use of metaphors drawn from that background.

In the earlier discussion the remedy for sin (and, by analogy, for redefined impurity) was demonstrated to be non-ritualistic and, therefore, non-magical. As the only non-magical alternative, the weak group, weak grid cosmology matches the perspective of the implied society on the issue of magic.

The Individual and Society

Despite the communal emphasis in Hebrews, no subservience of the individual to the society is evident, as would be expected in a strong group, strong grid society.[71] Exhortations, instructions, and warnings addressed to individuals as members of a community are identifiable. Having an 'evil heart of unbelief' (3.12) is portrayed as an individual issue (ἐν τινι ὑμῶν ['in any of you']), as are hardening (presumably of the heart; 3.13; a problem related to τις ἐξ ὑμῶν ['any of you']) and 'falling short' (4.1; τις ἐξ ὑμῶν). The positive examples of faithfulness are individuals[72] (Heb. 11; note especially the example of Moses, an individual who chose to join 'the people of God'; 11.24-25), while the most prominent negative example is a group (τῇ γενεᾷ ταύτῃ ['this generation']; 3.10).

Members are directed to exhort one another (παρακαλεῖτε ἑαυτοὺς ['exort one another'], 3:13) and are encouraged to be concerned about one another (κατανοῶμεν ἀλλήλους ['consider one another'], 10.24).

---

69. Isenberg and Owen, 'Bodies, Natural and Contrived', p. 7.
70. Isenberg and Owen, 'Bodies, Natural and Contrived', p. 8.
71. Isenberg and Owen, 'Bodies, Natural and Contrived', p. 7.
72. Eisenbaum (*The Jewish Heroes of Christian History*, p. 178) described the exemplars of faith as 'marginalized individuals who are portrayed as standing outside the nation of Israel.'

Such commitment to the community is more principled than the 'pragmatic and adaptable' approach of the weak group, strong grid cosmology.[73] No evidence from Hebrews can be cited for confused roles or for a 'distinction between appearance and internal state',[74] so the strong group, weak grid cosmology is not evident as the implicit view of the author.

The weak group, weak grid cosmology demonstrates 'no antagonism between society and self...roles [are] rejected, self-control and social control [are] low'.[75] Conflict between self and community is absent from the implied society, though the actual practice of some members of the congregation may betray a lack of commitment ('not forsaking the gathering together of yourselves, as is the custom of some', 10.25). In the earlier discussion of grid strength, the absence of strictly defined roles was noted. Self-control is not a prominent issue in Hebrews and the primary form of social control is expressed in terms of accountability to and discipline by God, not to or by other (human) members of the society (2.1-4; 4.12-13; 10.26-31; 12.5-11, 25; 13.17). Of the four alternatives, the weak group, weak grid cosmology correlates most fully with the individual's position in the implied society.

The Body

In Hebrews language referring to the body is not employed symbolically. The words 'flesh' and 'body' occur as metaphors for the incarnation (σάρξ, 2.14; 5.17; σῶμα, 10.5), for Jesus' self-sacrifice (σάρξ, 10.20; σῶμα, 10.5, 10), for the external aspects of the law (σάρξ, 9.10, 13, contrasted with the conscience in both instances), for humanity (σάρξ, 12.9, 'fathers according to the flesh'), and for physical presence (σῶμα, 13.3, 'as being with them in body'). Literal usages of σῶμα include a baptismal allusion (10.22) and a reference to the Yom Kippur sacrificial victims (13.11). The non-symbolic nature of the body is evident in the author's failure to note the unclean status of the bodies of these animals and in his similar silence with reference to the 'corpses [that] fell in the wilderness' (3.17). In no instance was the body employed as a negative image.

The author demonstrated neither excessive concern with the body nor avoidance of 'body' language. Occurrences in Hebrews of the various

73. Isenberg and Owen, 'Bodies, Natural and Contrived', p. 8.
74. Isenberg and Owen, 'Bodies, Natural and Contrived', p. 7.
75. Isenberg and Owen, 'Bodies, Natural and Contrived', p. 8.

New Testament terms for the body (3.95% of the total New Testament occurrences) are in proportion to the length of the epistle compared to the entire New Testament (3.57%). Frequency of 'body' language in Hebrews is significantly less than in the Pauline corpus (figure 5).

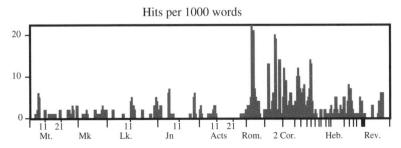

Figure 5. *New Testament frequency of occurrence for κῶλον, πτῶμα, σάρξ, σκεῦος, σκῆνος, σκήνωμα, σῶμα, σωματικός, σωματικῶς, and ὁ ἔξω ἄνθρωπος*

No tight control of the body is evident, so the strong group, strong grid option can be rejected. Since the body is not under attack the strong group, weak grid alternative is dismissed. Discerning between the two remaining choices is difficult, though based on the apparent lack of concern with the body the 'irrelevant' attitude of the weak group, weak grid cosmology may be more probable than the 'instrumental' approach of the weak group, strong grid cosmology.[76]

Personification of the Cosmos. Although the cosmos is not impersonal in Hebrews, the view of the cosmos is more consistent with the weak group, weak grid cosmology than with the other alternatives. Dualism, with 'warring forces of good and evil' is absent from the epistle, excluding the strong group, weak grid cosmology.[77] Angels are discussed prominently in the opening chapters, but they are subordinated to the Son and are mentioned only twice after Heb. 2.16 (12.22 and 13.2). The Devil is mentioned only once, and is described not as the personification of evil but as the one who holds the power of death over humanity (2.14). Several interpreters have read the phrase 'the one having the power of death, namely the devil' (2.14) as a reference to the leader of the powers of evil,[78] but such interpretations are derived more

---

76. Isenberg and Owen, 'Bodies, Natural and Contrived', pp. 7-8.
77. Isenberg and Owen, 'Bodies, Natural and Contrived', p. 8.
78. Gustaf Aulén, *Christus Victor: An Historical Study of the Three Main Types*

from other New Testament texts than from Hebrews; the author did not grant explicitly that title to the Devil.

Also absent from Hebrews is the strong group, weak grid perception of an unjust, whimsical universe.[79] Again, the hypothesis that the implied society is weak group, weak grid is a plausible explanation for this absence.

Lack of mediation, a characteristic of the paradigmatic weak group, weak grid cosmology,[80] is modified in the implied society. Christ functions as a mediator (7.25; 9.24), yet the believer is able to 'approach the throne of grace with boldness' (4.16) and has 'confidence to enter the sanctuary with the blood of Jesus' (10.19). Nothing in Hebrews contradicts the strong group, strong grid view of the cosmos, which is 'anthropomorphic; non-dualistic;...just and non-capricious',[81] though the privilege of free access to God that is granted to believers supports the conclusion that the implied society has a weak group, weak grid cosmology.

The greatest discrepancy between the personification of the cosmos in the implied society and the weak group, weak grid cosmology is the paradigmatic tendency to favor an impersonal cosmos. With a strong theistic/christological view of the cosmos (Christ seated at the right hand of God), the implied society views the cosmic powers as personal (perhaps even anthropomorphic) beings. This perspective reflects the Jewish/Old Testament roots of Christianity, and is a cherished artifact of the community from which the author and his readers emerged. Because of the author's depiction of God and Christ, the weak group, strong grid view of 'God as junior partner'[82] can be dismissed summarily.

Suffering and Misfortune
The author of Hebrews viewed the believers' suffering and misfortune as identification with Jesus (13.13), who himself was perfected, tested,

of the Idea of Atonement (trans. A.G. Hebert; New York: Collier Books, Macmillan Publishing Company, 1986), pp. 4, 77; John McRay, 'Atonement and Apocalyptic in the Book of Hebrews', *ResQ* 23 (1980), pp. 1-9 (4); John T. Carroll and Joel B. Green, *The Death of Jesus in Early Christianity* (Peabody, MA: Hendrickson, 1995), p. 137; Attridge, *Hebrews*, p. 92; Ellingworth, *Hebrews*, p. 173.
    79. Isenberg and Owen, 'Bodies, Natural and Contrived', p. 8.
    80. Isenberg and Owen, 'Bodies, Natural and Contrived', p. 8.
    81. Isenberg and Owen, 'Bodies, Natural and Contrived', p. 7.
    82. Isenberg and Owen, 'Bodies, Natural and Contrived', p. 8.

and taught obedience through suffering (2.10, 18; 5.8). In the most sustained discussion of the subject (12.1-11), suffering is equated with the discipline of a loving father. In that discussion, the author quoted approvingly Prov. 3.11-12:

> For whom the Lord loves he disciplines,
>   and he punishes every son whom he accepts (12.6).

This proverb is reflective of a weak group, weak grid perception that 'love conquers all'.[83]

When contrasted with the other cosmological alternatives, this weak group, weak grid explanation for suffering and misfortune is the only reasonable match to the view presented in Hebrews. In a strong group, strong grid society, suffering and misfortune are 'the result of automatic punishment for the violation of formal rules'.[84] The author subordinated the view of sin implied in that explanation to an interiorized view of sin and viewed suffering positively as discipline, not negatively as punishment. Suffering as the result of 'unjust' acts by 'malevolent forces', the explanation offered in strong group, weak grid societies[85] is foreign to the author's counsel to accept discipline (12.7). Similarly, the acceptance of discipline is contradictory to the weak group, strong grid perception that 'an intelligent person ought to be able to avoid' suffering and misfortune.[86]

The Coherence of the Cosmology of the Implied Society

The discussion of the cosmology of the implied society is summarized in table 7. Only the weak group, weak grid paradigmatic cosmology is consistent with the implicit cosmology of the implied society with respect to all eight parameters examined. The most clearly excluded cosmology is the strong group, strong grid alternative, the cosmology associated with the type of society from which the author and his readers withdrew (i.e. first-century CE hellenistic Judaism) when they joined the new covenant community.

Three parameters exhibit probable agreement with the weak group, weak grid paradigm rather than strong agreement: personal identity, body, and personification of the cosmos. For two of these parameters

---

83. Isenberg and Owen, 'Bodies, Natural and Contrived', p. 8.
84. Isenberg and Owen, 'Bodies, Natural and Contrived', p. 7.
85. Isenberg and Owen, 'Bodies, Natural and Contrived', p. 8.
86. Isenberg and Owen, 'Bodies, Natural and Contrived', p. 8.

(personal identity and body) the lower level of confidence reflects the limited information available in Hebrews. The lower confidence for the personification of the cosmos reflects the strongly theistic/christological stance of the author.

Two important conclusions can be drawn from this information. First, the cosmology of the implied society is coherent; the implicit cosmology can be reconciled with one and only one of the paradigmatic cosmologies. Second, the implicit cosmology of the ideal society matches the cosmology predicted by a direct assessment of the implicit group and grid characteristics of that society, i.e., the paradigmatic weak group, weak grid cosmology. The coherence of the implicit cosmology and the match between the predicted cosmology and the implicit cosmology support the validity of Douglas's group/grid paradigm in the examination of the sociological function of the critique of the levitical system in the epistle to the Hebrews.

Table 7. *The coherence of the cosmology of the implied society*

	A Weak Group Strong Grid	B Weak Group Weak Grid	C Strong Group Strong Grid	D Strong Group Weak Grid
Purity	–	•	X	X
Ritual	–/x	•	X	X
Magic	–	•	X	X
Personal identity	–/x	○	X	–
Body	–	○	X	X
Trance		No	Data	
Sin	–/x	•	X	–/x
Personification of the cosmos	X	○	–	X
Suffering and misfortune	X	•	X	X

Key

•	=	strong agreement
○	=	probable agreement
X	=	excluded
–	=	unclear or ambiguous

Chapter 5

THE SOCIOLOGICAL FUNCTION OF THE CRITIQUE
OF THE LEVITICAL SYSTEM

Cosmologies and Persuasion

'Symbols can be rejected, they can be changed, but we cannot do without symbols altogether. Anyone challenging authority should challenge its particular symbols and find new symbols so as to pit against one discarded form of expression another at least as coherent.'[1] In the levitical system first-century Judaism possessed a symbolically-oriented structure that defined and reinforced first-century Jewish society. The embedded symbols revolved around the hierarchical priesthood, the sacred space of the sanctuary, the necessity of cultic purity, the Law as arbiter of sin, and the sacrificial ritual as remedy for sin. By challenging the levitical system, the author of Hebrews challenged the 'particular symbols' of first-century Judaism. The levitical priesthood is dethroned from its noble status, the Holy of Holies is no longer an exclusively hieratic precinct, sin as a forensic matter is subordinated to internal, ethical issues of the conscience, and the inefficacy of the levitical sacrifices is declared emphatically. By challenging the undergirding symbols of first-century Judaism, the author set the stage for the definition of a new society.

As expected in Douglas's paradigm, the author offered a new set of symbols, constructing a new, coherent 'form of expression'. In place of the levitical nobility, 'we have a high priest' (8.1) who sits at the right hand of God. 'We have an altar' (13.10) where the perfect, once-for-all sacrifice for sin has been offered. Though no earthly sanctuary stands as a magnet, drawing the members together, the community's perfect high priest ministers in the true, greater, and more perfect sanctuary (8.2; 12.11), a sanctuary to which believers have access (10.19; cf. 4.16;

---

1. Douglas, *Natural Symbols*, p. xxii.

6.19-20). Other symbols in the new, ideal, implied society include the city (11.11, 16; 12.22; 13.14), the kingdom (12.28), and Mt Zion (12.22). The coherence of the implied society's cosmology, the structure into which these new symbols fit, has been demonstrated in the previous chapter.

With this coherent, rich, alternative set of symbols, the author has avoided a peril about which Douglas warned: 'the early stages of revolt are generally incoherent, and one of the natural symbolic forces in this particular contrast is a protest against symbolisation as such, a plain vote for incoherence. In those angry times, instead of arguing about how authority should be redefined, much energy went into arguing against definition or against form of any kind'.[2] Douglas suggested that, in such an environment, brute force takes the place of symbol-based persuasion.[3] By presenting the new symbols as superior alternatives to the old, the author opted for persuasive rhetoric rather than coercion in his appeal to the congregation.

Appreciation of this persuasive function of the new symbolic structure aids recognition of the interaction between the doctrinal and hortatory sections of Hebrews.[4] The critique of the levitical system is presented primarily in the cultic section of the epistle (7.1–10.18), the longest doctrinal argument in Hebrews. In this extended discussion the alternative sin concept and the transcendence of ritual are established. Having argued implicitly for an alternative cosmology (the weak group, weak grid cosmology of the implied society versus the strong group, strong grid cosmology of Judaism), the author employed the embedded symbols of the new cosmology in his transition to exhortation:

> Therefore, brothers [and sisters], since we have boldness to enter *the sanctuary* by *the blood of Jesus, a new and living way through the curtain, that is his flesh,* having been inaugurated, and [having] *a great priest over the house of God,* let us approach with true hearts in full assurance of faith, *hearts having been sprinkled from an evil conscience* and bodies having been washed with pure water; let us hold fast to the

2.   Douglas, *Natural Symbols*, p. xxii.
3.   Douglas, *Natural Symbols*, p. xxii.
4.   The relationship between exposition and paraenesis in Hebrews has been discussed widely. For recent treatments, see George H. Guthrie, *The Structure of Hebrews: A Text-Linguistic Analysis* (NovTSup; Leiden: E.J. Brill, 1994), pp. 112-47; Steve Stanley, 'The Structure of Hebrews from Three Perspectives', *TynBul* 45 (1994), pp. 250-51, 262-63; cf. Attridge, *Hebrews*, pp. 15, 21; Ellingworth, *Hebrews*, p. 58.

confession of hope without wavering, for the one who promised is faithful, and let us consider how to stimulate one another to love and good works, not forsaking the gathering together of yourselves, as is the custom of some, but encouraging [one another], and so much more since you see the day approaching (10.19-25; emphasis mine).

The perfect self-sacrifice of Christ ('a great priest'), the believers' access to the true sanctuary ('boldness to enter the sanctuary', 'a new and living way through the curtain...having been inaugurated'), and the resolution of the fundamental problem of sin ('hearts having been sprinkled from an evil conscience') constitute the basis upon which the appeal is grounded. These symbols derived from doctrinal arguments are presented to motivate the readers to faithfulness in the new covenant community. As George Guthrie stated, 'the expositional material serves the hortatory purpose of the whole work. The exposition...does more than theologically inform; it offers a powerful motivation for active obedience and endurance in the race toward the lasting city.'[5]

Recognition of the rhetorical potential of the symbols derived from the critique of the levitical system leads to the question: of what and/or to what is the author seeking to persuade his audience? Before addressing this question, a brief examination of alternative evaluations of the levitical system in *1 Clem.* and in the Qumran library will prove informative.

Alternative Evaluations of the Levitical System

Evaluations of the levitical system in *1 Clem.* and in the Qumran Rules are relevant to the present study for two reasons: (1) both *1 Clem.* and the community represented in the Qumran corpus have been associated with the Epistle to the Hebrews and (2) the evaluations of the levitical system in *1 Clem.* and in the Qumran Rules serve explicitly social functions. By examining these alternative approaches, the critique presented in Hebrews can be viewed in a larger context than that provided by an examination of Hebrews alone.

1 Clement
Eusebius implied a relationship between Hebrews and *1 Clem.* when he noted that some Christians attributed the authorship of Hebrews to

5. Guthrie, *The Structure of Hebrews*, pp. 143-45.

'Clement, who was bishop of the Romans'.[6] Although this identification of the author is unlikely,[7] the dependance of *1 Clem.* on Hebrews is clear.[8]

(Re)establishment of order and of peace within the church are the complementary purposes of *1 Clem.*[9] A thorough assessment of the character of the community being advocated in *1 Clem.* is beyond the scope of the present discussion, though a sketch of the sociology/ecclesiology of the letter is possible.[10] According to the spokesman of the Roman congregation, the church is God's 'own special people',[11] having been 'called and sanctified by the will of God'.[12] The boundary between the church and outsiders is drawn more distinctly in *1 Clem.* than in Hebrews. Antagonists are described as opponents of God[13] (as in Hebrews), but also (unlike Hebrews) as foes of the congregation: 'those who exalt themselves over his [Christ's] flock', usurpers of the position of 'righteous people', and torturers of 'those who served God with a holy and blameless resolve'.[14] These comments suggest that the community from which *1 Clem.* originated was a strong group society. James Jeffers concluded that the congregation reflected in *1 Clem.* originated as a sect but, by the time the epistle was composed, had evolved into a community more confident of its unique identity in the larger world.[15]

An appeal to the natural order supports the conclusion that *1 Clem.*

6.   Eusebius, *Ecclesiastical History* 6.25.14.

7.   Ellingworth, *Hebrews*, p. 13.

8.   Ellingworth, *Hebrews*, p. 29; Attridge, *Hebrews*, pp. 6-7; Bruce, *Hebrews*, pp. 20-21; Buchanan, *To the Hebrews*, p. 261; Lane, *Hebrews 1–8*, pp. lxii-lxiii.

9.   Clayton N. Jefford, *Reading the Apostolic Fathers: An Introduction* (Peabody, MA: Hendrickson, 1996), pp. 105-106.

10.   For a more thorough sociological examination of *1 Clem.*, cf. James S. Jeffers, *Conflict at Rome: Social Order and Hierarchy in Early Christianity* (Minneapolis: Fortress Press, 1991).

11.   *1 Clem.* 64. All quotations from *1 Clement* are from *The Apostolic Fathers: Greek Texts and English Translations of Their Writings* (J. B. Lightfoot, J. R. Harmer and Michael W. Holmes [eds. and trans.]; Grand Rapids, MI: Baker Book House, 2nd edn, 1992).

12.   *1 Clem.* epistolary prefix; cf. 1.1; 6.1; 32.4; 65.2.

13.   *1 Clem.* 35.6; 36.6.

14.   *1 Clem.* 16.1; 45.3, 7.

15.   Jeffers, *Conflict at Rome*, p. 186.

reflects a strong group orientation.[16] 'Clement's intention is to show from the examples that the established order in nature serves as an ideal pattern of God's perfect rule, a model for the church to emulate. Every natural phenomenon operates just as God commands it. It follows then that every deviation from the appointed course or order—and it is as true in the church as it is in the natural world—is a violation of God's command and constitutes an act of disobedience to his will.'[17] One aspect of creation noted in *1 Clem.* is that 'having already created the sea and the living creatures in it, he fixed its boundaries by his own power... So, since we have this pattern, let us unhesitatingly conform ourselves to his will; let us with all our strength do the work of righteousness.'[18] Such imagery, affirming an inviolable boundary, is alien to Hebrews, but is consistent with a strong group society.

Positive use of boundary imagery is likewise consistent with a strong grid society, indicators of which are explicit in *1 Clem.* In 'one of the earliest surviving expressions of the notion of "apostolic succession" ',[19] the author of *1 Clem.* established a line of authority from God to Jesus Christ, who appointed the apostles, who themselves appointed bishops and deacons (*1 Clem.* 42). The fact that these latter offices have 'a permanent character', being transferred to another only upon the death of the holder confirms the strong grid character of the society being defined (*1 Clem.* 44.2). The author of *1 Clem.* employed an analogy to the Roman military hierarchy to justify order in the church (*1 Clem.* 37.1-4). Jeffers described the leadership of the church according to *1 Clem.* as 'an elite, self-appointed group, separate from and not directly answerable to the larger membership, which performed its functions blamelessly and without the assistance of the common members'.[20]

16. Douglas ('Cultural Bias', p. 211); 'The uses of nature in moral justification are all-pervasive' in strong group, strong grid societies. 'This is the social context in which theories of Natural Law flourish.'

17. D.W.F. Wong, 'Natural and Divine Order in 1 Clement', *VC* 31 (1977), pp. 81-87 (81-82).

18. *1 Clem.* 33.3, 8. Neither the fixing of the boundaries nor the verb ἐγκλείω (used in *1 Clem.*) is present in the Septuagint account of Creation in Gen. 1–2. Interestingly, the only occurrence of ἐγκλείω in the LXX is in Ezek. 3.24, the work of an author with pronounced priestly/cultic interests.

19. Bart D. Ehrman, *The New Testament: A Historical Introduction to the Early Christian Writings* (New York: Oxford University Press, 1997), p. 391.

20. Jeffers, *Conflict at Rome*, p. 174.

Cosmological aspects of *1 Clem.* confirm the strong group, strong grid character of the society being defined. Obedience to God is viewed primarily in legal terms (employing δικαίωμα, 'regulation', ἐντολή, 'commandment', νόμιμος, 'statute', παράγγελμα, 'order', and πρόσταγμα, 'injunction' to refer to expressions of God's will).[21] The body is employed as a positive image of the community (*1 Clem.* 37.5; 46.7)). As noted above, the cosmos is orderly and behaves according to the design of a benevolent creator (*1 Clem.* 20), while personified forces of evil are relegated to a minor role ((*1 Clem.* 51.1). Concern about schism, more common in strong group, weak grid societies, is modified by a desire to lead the schismatics to repentance, reintegrating them into the community,[22] rather than to expel them.

With this social orientation, an acceptance of ritual within the community should be expected and any evaluation of the levitical cultus should be positive. Both of these characteristics are present in *1 Clem.* An early indication of the positive treatment of the cultus occurs in the mention of Jesus' ancestry. Whereas the author of Hebrews noted Jesus' non-priestly lineage, the distinct lines of descent are obscured in *1 Clem.*: 'For from Jacob come all the priests and Levites who minister at the altar of God; from him comes the Lord Jesus according to the flesh' (*1 Clem.* 32.2). Identifying Jesus as high priest can, therefore, be viewed as consistent with the grid of Judaism as portrayed in *1 Clem.*, not as a challenge to that grid (*1 Clem.* 36.1; 61.3; 64).

Explicit discussion of the levitical system is present in *1 Clem.* 40–41. In that presentation the sacred status of times and locations, the hierarchy within the levitical priesthood, and the distinction between priests and laity are affirmed. Application of that discussion to the situation of the readers begins in *1 Clem.* 40 and continues through *1 Clem.* 44. Extending the validity of the principles discovered in the levitical system, the author of *1 Clem.* defended the hierarchical status of apostles, bishops, and deacons (also identifying the latter category [or categories] as presbyters).

Worship in the church is portrayed in ritualistic terms based on the discussion of the levitical cultus. 'We ought to do, in order, everything that the Master has commanded us to perform at the appointed times… Let each of you, brothers, in his proper order give thanks [εὐχαριστείτω] to God, maintaining a good conscience, not overstep-

---

21. *1 Clem.* 2.8; 3.4; 13.3; 58.2.
22. *1 Clem.* 14.3; 51.1; 54.1-4; 56.1; 57.1-2; 58.2; 63.2.

ping the designated rule of his ministry, but acting with reverence... For it will be no small sin for us, if we depose from the bishop's office those who have offered the gifts blamelessly and in holiness [τοὺς ἀμέμπτως καὶ ὁσίως προσενεγκόντας τὰ δῶρα]' (*1 Clem.* 40.1; 41.1; 44.4). Georges Blond commented:

> Even if Clement does not use the terms that later became technical designations for the eucharist, the reality is present in the letter as far as the sacrificial aspect of the eucharist is concerned. It is spoken of as having replaced the various sacrifices of the Old Testament and thus as being itself a sacrifice. It has been instituted by the Lord and is closely connected with the hierarchy, whose essential function it is to offer sacrifices.
>
> The principal act of the Mosaic cultus was the offering of sacrifices in accordance with a minutely detailed set of ritual prescriptions; it follows that the principal act of New Testament worship is likewise a sacrifice.[23]

Though more concise, Robert Grant reached a similar conclusion: 'Clement uses the sacrificial ordinances of the Old Testament to prepare the ground for his defense of ordinances (which he must regard as analogous) in regard to the Church.'[24] These comments are valid assessments of the positive critique of the levitical system in *1 Clem.*

The Qumran Rules

Numerous connections between Hebrews and the Qumran documents have been claimed. Ceslas Spicq found similarities between the epistle and the *Damascus Document* and other Qumran texts, leading him to suggest that the recipients of Hebrews included 'a certain number of ex-Qumranians'.[25] Proposed correlations between the Qumran corpus and

---

23. Georges Blond, 'Clement of Rome', in Raymond Johanny (ed.), *The Eucharist of the Early Christians* (trans. Matthew J. O'Connell; New York: Pueblo Publishing Company, 1978), pp. 25, 29.

24. Robert M. Grant commenting on *1 Clement* in *The Apostolic Fathers: A New Translation and Commentary*. II. *First and Second Clement* (trans. Holt H. Graham, introduction and commentary by Robert M. Grant; New York: Thomas Nelson and Sons, 1965), p. 69.

25. Ceslas Spicq, 'L'épitre aux Hébreux, Apollos, Jean-Baptiste, les Hellénistes et Qumran', *RevQ* 1 (1959): pp. 365-90 (371, 390). Spicq stated: 'Tout s'expliquerait au mieux si Apollos s'adressait à des esséno-chrétiens, à des prêtres juifs—parmi lesquels pouvait se trouver un certain nombre d'ex-qumrâniens—et dont il connait la formation doctrinale et biblique, les préoccupations spirituelles, les "préjugés" religieux.'

the Epistle to the Hebrews include the idea of the congregation as the new covenant community, the concept of a priestly messiah, and the interest in Melchizedek.[26] Though any assertions of the conceptual dependance of Hebrews on Qumran theology are unwarranted,[27] the similarities validate a consideration in the present study of the Qumran critique of the sacrificial cultus.

Isenberg and Owen commented that 'one could hardly imagine a community that would score higher on group and grid than Qumran'.[28] A full group/grid assessment of the Qumran community is outside the confines of the present task, though the outlines of such an analysis can be summarized.

Based on data present in the defining Rules of the community, the society at Qumran can be classified as strong group, strong grid. Group strength is most evident in the well-defined and well-defended boundary separating members from non-members (corresponding to Gross and Rayner's 'impermeability' predicate),[29] with internal group cohesion reinforced by regular communal activities (e.g. the communal meals and the meetings of the Council of the Community, both described in 1QS 6.2-3, indicative of high values for proximity and transitivity).[30] Isolation from outsiders was a tenet of life at Qumran,[31] limiting severely interactions between members and nonmembers (suggesting

---

26. Lane, *Hebrews 1–8*; p. cviii.
27. Lane, *Hebrews 1–8*; p. cviii.
28. Isenberg and Owen, 'Bodies, Natural and Contrived', p. 11.
29. Gross and Rayner, *Measuring Culture*, p. 78.
30. Gross and Rayner, *Measuring Culture*, pp. 73-77.
31. Cf. requirements to 'keep apart from men of sin' (1QS 5.1-2), to avoid confusing their goods with 'men of deceit' (1QS 9.8), to avoid arguments with 'the men of the pit' (1QS 9.16; 10.19), to feel 'everlasting hatred for the men of the pit' (1QS 9.21-22), 'to separate themselves from the sons of the pit' (CD 6.14-15), and to avoid 'gentiles' on the sabbath (CD 6.14-15). All quotations from the Qumran texts are from Florentino García Martínez and Wilfred G.E. Watson (eds. and trans.), *The Dead Sea Scrolls Translated: The Qumran Texts in English* (Leiden: E.J. Brill; Grand Rapids: Eerdmans, 2nd edn, 1996). Transcriptions of the original Qumran texts are based on James H. Charlesworth (ed.), *The Dead Sea Scrolls: Hebrew, Aramaic, and Greek Texts with English Translations*. I. *Rule of the Community and Related Documents* (Tübingen: J.C.B. Mohr [Paul Siebeck]; Louisville: Westminster John Knox Press, 1995) and II. *Damascus Document, War Scroll, and Related Documents* (Tübingen: J.C.B. Mohr [Paul Siebeck]; Louisville: Westminster John Knox Press, 1995).

high values for the frequency and scope predicates).[32]

Status within the community was subject to change, but a fixed hierarchy based on ancestry was in place: chief priests, other priests, the Messiah, levites/elders, Israelites, proselytes.[33] Nowhere do the texts suggest that the annual realignment could override this inherent, immutable structure. With the assignment of status came authority; junior members were obligated to obey their seniors.[34] In this setting specialization, entitlement, and asymmetry are high.[35] This internal structure was supplemented by strict accountability within the community,[36] confirming Qumran as a strong grid society.[37]

Qumran matched the paradigmatic strong group, strong grid cosmology on most points. Purity was a major concern,[38] much of the sectarians' activity can be described as ritualistic,[39] the emphasis on community suggests that individual identity was subordinated to group identity,[40] the body was controlled strictly,[41] the primary sin was forensic (failure to submit to the covenant as defined by the community, supported by detailed lists of specific infractions and corresponding punishments[42]), and a just God was responsible for rewards and punish-

32. Gross and Rayner, *Measuring Culture*, pp. 77-78.

33. 1QS 6.8-9; CD 14.3-5; 1QSa 2.12-18.

34. 1QS 5.15-16, 23; 6.2.

35. Gross and Rayner, *Measuring Culture*, pp. 79-81.

36. 1QS 6.24-9.2; CD 9.1-22; 12.2-6; 14.20-22; 15.1-5.

37. Gross and Rayner, *Measuring Culture*, pp. 81-82.

38. 1QS 5.13-14; 6.16-21; CD 5.6-7; 6.14-18; 10.10-12.2).

39. E.g. ritual immersions, communal meals, and the enigmatic deposits of bones at the sectarian center. On the last of these cf J.-B. Humbert, 'L'espace sacré à Qumrân: Propositions pour l'Archéologie', *RB* 101 (1994), pp. 161-214 (205); Lawrence H. Schiffman, 'Communal Meals at Qumran', *RevQ* 10 (1979), pp. 45-56 (48-49).

40. Cf. the frequent references to the יחד and to the רבים in the Rules.

41. Among the regulations of the community were prohibitions of public nudity (1QS 7.14-16) and spitting during a meeting (1QS 7.15; cf. Josephus, *War* 2.147 with reference to the Essenes). Pollution of the temple by menstrual blood and by sexual activity within the holy city was a prominent concern of the sectarians (CD 5.6-7; 12.1-2). In the eschatalogical community, 'everyone who is defiled in his flesh, paralysed in his feet or in his hands, lame, blind, deaf, dumb or defiled in his flesh with a blemish visible to the eyes, or the tottering old man who cannot keep upright in the midst of the assembly' was excluded from the communal gathering (1QSa 2.4-8).

42. 1QS 6.24-9.2; CD 9.1, 16-22; 12.2-6; 14.20-22; 15.1-5. The caution that

ments.[43] The two most noteworthy variations from the pure strong group, strong grid pattern were the rejection of the Jerusalem cultus and the perception of a dualistic cosmos.

Cosmological dualism is uncharacteristic of strong group, strong grid societies.[44] The presence of dualism in the implicit cosmology of the Qumran Rules requires either a modification to the paradigm or a plausible explanation for this peculiarity. James Charlesworth has offered a plausible explanation. Although the Qumran sectarians were dualistic in their attitude toward the cosmos, their dualism was modified by a strict monotheism where the entire cosmos was viewed as subject ultimately to God.[45] While still a deviation from the pure strong group, strong grid cosmology, the dualism of Qumran does not represent a violation of the paradigm.

Rejection of the Jerusalem cultus contrasted with the generally ritualistic nature of life in the Qumran community. Ritualized meals reinforced the grid of the society.[46] Citing *The Community Rule* (1QS) 6.6-8, Steven Fraade stated that 'ongoing study was a ritualized part of the community's collective life'.[47] Immersion for purification was another prominent ritual in the community. An explanation for the rejection of the Jerusalem cultus must account for the otherwise ritualistic nature of Qumran life.

The required explanation comes in the recognition that the Qumran community had rejected the sacrificial cultus *as practiced by the Jerusalem-based priesthood*. No absolute rejection of a sacrificial cult or of all ritual was implied or intended in the denunciation of the contemporary Jerusalem temple liturgy. 'The Essenes had rejected and condemned a clergy that was illegitimate in their eyes, an irregular cult

---

'no-one should defile his soul with any living being or one which creeps, by eating them' (CD 12.11-12) constitutes strong evidence that any internalized sense of sin was subordinated to the external, forensic view.

43. 1QS 1.10-11; 2.8-9, 15-16; 4.18-19; 10.18, 20, 25; 11.10, 12, 15; CD 1.21-2.1; 3.8-9; 5.15-16; 8.2-3.

44. Isenberg and Owen, 'Bodies, Natural and Contrived', p. 7.

45. James H. Charlesworth, 'A Critical Comparison of the Dualism in 1QS 3:13-4:26 and the 'Dualism' Contained in the Gospel of John', in James H. Charlesworth (ed.), *John and the Dead Sea Scrolls* (New York: Crossroad, 1991), pp. 76-106 (88-89).

46. 1QS 6.5; 1QSa 2.11-22.

47. Steven D. Fraade, 'Interpretive Authority in the Studying Community at Qumran', *JJS* 44 (Spring 1993), pp. 46-69 (56).

and a holy place profaned by the practices of its priests, but they had not denied the principle of the Temple and they maintained the hope of a restoration of the true cult'.[48]

One phrase in *The Community Rule* is similar cosmetically to a comment in the concluding paragraphs of Hebrews. In their isolation from the temple cultus, the Qumran sectarians found promise of atonement in 'the offering of the lips [תרומת שפתים]' (1QS 9.4-5). Although this expression resembles Heb. 13:15 ('a sacrifice of praise to God, which is the fruit of lips confessing his name'), the *Rule* adds 'in compliance with the decree [למשפט]' (1QS 9.5), giving the expression a more ritualistic connotation than is present in Hebrews.

With their repudiation of the Jerusalem cultus the Qumran sectarians were not seeking to define a more open, inclusive society. On the contrary, one of their objections was that the Jerusalem cultus was too accessible to gentiles: 'No-one should sell an animal, or a clean bird, to the gentiles lest they sacrifice them. And he should not sell them anything from his granary or his press, at any price' (CD 12.8-10). Though these restrictions could be viewed as a measure to impede pagan sacrifices,[49] another legal document included a more explicit prohibition denying to gentiles even indirect access to the temple cultus: '[None] of the wheat of the Gentiles shall be brought into the temple' (4QMMT 8).[50] In their critique of the sacrificial cult, the Qumran sectarians sought to define themselves as 'a closed community governed by stricter rules for worship, daily life, and possible warfare'.[51]

Society and Cult in 1 Clement and in the Qumran Rules
Examined in detail, the critiques of the Jerusalem cultus in *1 Clem.* and in the Qumran Rules differ significantly. The Qumran texts predate the Roman destruction of the temple, were composed by members of an

48. André Caquot, 'La secte de Qoumrân et le temple (essai de synthèse)', *RHPR* 72 (1992), pp. 3-14 (3); 'Les Esséniens ont rejeté et condamné un clergé illégitime à leurs yeux, un culte irrégulier et un lieu saint profané par les pratiques de ses prêtres, mais ils n'ont pas renié le principe du Temple et ont entretenu l'espérance d'une restauration du vrai culte.' Cf. Ellingworth, *Hebrews*, p. 48; Walker, *Jesus and the Holy City*, p. 207.

49. Lawrence H. Schiffman, *Reclaiming the Dead Sea Scrolls: The History of Judaism, the Background of Christianity, The Lost Library of Qumran* (Philadelphia: Jewish Publication Society, 1994), pp. 372-73.

50. Cf. Schiffman, *Reclaiming the Dead Sea Scrolls*, p. 379.

51. Ellingworth, *Hebrews*, p. 48.

isolationist sect within Judaism, and presented a scathing rejection of the active, contemporary cult. Conversely, *1 Clem.* was composed after the destruction of the temple (c. 95–96 CE, and probably not before 80 CE according to most interpreters[52]), reflects a community that was increasingly mixed (Jewish and gentile) and increasingly confident in its interaction with the Greco-Roman world, and affirmed the principles underlying the (now terminated) Jerusalem cultus (mentioning Jerusalem specifically in *1 Clem.* 41.2).

The significance of these alternative critiques to a study of the comparable material in Hebrews resides in their diversity. In Hebrews the sacrificial system is never employed as the model for the implied society (as in *1 Clem.*) nor is the cultus vilified (as in the charge that the Jerusalem priests knowingly and willingly defiled the sanctuary, an accusation made in *The Damascus Document* (CD) 5.6-7). The author of Hebrews viewed the cultus as appropriate in its age ('until the time of setting right'; 9.10) , but as having been fulfilled and brought to a conclusion by the sacrifice of Jesus 'once at the consummation of the ages' (9.26). Hebrews, then, represents a third, distinct, alternative view of the levitical cultus, neither conformist nor acrimonious, but, in its own manner, more revolutionary than either.

Despite the many differences between *1 Clem.* and the Qumran library, the two treatments of the Jerusalem cult have a similar function: to validate and to reinforce a particular type of society. The Qumran Rules 'serve to establish the group or groups for which they were intended'.[53] Denunciation of the contemporary cultus contributed to this sociological end by exemplifying the issues that resulted in the separation of the sectarians from the majority of Jewish society. That a complex of issues related to the temple and to the sanctity of Jerusalem as a whole were central in the definition of Qumran identity is most clear in *The Halakhic Letter* (4QMMT).[54]

A 'detestable and unholy schism' involving the removal from office of the presbyters by (a faction) within the congregation at Corinth provoked the writing of *1 Clem.* (*1 Clem.* 1.1; 44.6; 47.6). Having invoked the example of the levitical system, the Roman spokesman defined the proper order of Christian society: ' "Only let the flock of Christ be at

---

52. Laurence L. Welborn, 'Clement, First Epistle of', ABD, I, pp. 1055-60 (1060).

53. García Martínez, *The Dead Sea Scrolls Translated*, p. 2.

54. Schiffman, *Reclaiming the Dead Sea Scrolls*, p. 83.

peace with its duly appointed presbyters"... These are the things that those who live as citizens [οἱ πολιτευόμενοι] of the commonwealth of God [τὴν πολιτείαν τοῦ θεοῦ]—something not to be regretted—have done and will continue to do' (*1 Clem.* 54.2, 4). With the mention of the πολιτεία of God the sociological function of *1 Clem.* is explicit.

In these two widely divergent perspectives, the segregation of theology from sociology in analyses of critiques of the levitical system is unwarranted and unwise. The critiques are founded on theological convictions and are employed for sociological functions. Having demonstrated the validity of this principle in the cases of *1 Clem.* and the Qumran corpus, warrant is provided for an inquiry into the sociological function of the critique of the levitical system in Hebrews.

The Persuasive Goal: The Purpose of Hebrews

Whereas the sociological purposes of *1 Clem.* and of the Qumran Rules were explicit, the purpose of Hebrews is unstated and is, therefore, one of the 'puzzles' of Hebrews.[55] Because the critique of the levitical system is concentrated in the cultic section of the epistle (7.1–10.18) and that section comprises approximately 30 percent of the entire text, the purpose of Hebrews as a whole can be presumed reasonably to be related to the purpose of the levitical critique. This presumption is strengthened by the integration of exposition and exhortation in Hebrews. With the demonstration from related literature (*1 Clem.* and the Qumran documents) of a sociological function for critiques of the levitical cultus, the quest for the sociological function of the critique of the levitical system in Hebrews as a component of the overall purpose of the epistle is justified.

Lacking the explicit sociological clues of *1 Clem.* and the Qumran Rules, a less direct approach must be employed in identifying the socio- logical aims and intentions of the author of Hebrews. Following Doug- las's lead, the society implied in Hebrews has been categorized as weak group, weak grid, and the coherent cosmology of that society has been described. Further guidance is required to advance an hypothesis for the sociological function of the levitical critique and of the entire epistle.

A suggestion of an answer to the question of the sociological purpose of Hebrews is available in Douglas's further development of the group/ grid paradigm in her essay 'Cultural Bias'. In *Natural Symbols* her

---

55. Lane, *Hebrews 1–8*, p. xlvii.

attention was on cosmology, in the later study the focus was on culture, as stated in the title of the essay. Her goal in 'Cultural Bias' was to understand how the social environment relates to 'those beliefs and values which are derivable as justifications for action'; she sought to comprehend behaviors.[56] Included in the catalogue of behaviors were gardening, cooking, treatment of the old, treatment of those with handicaps, and punishment of offenders. Of the topics addressed in 'Cultural Bias', the one behavior most relevant to the study of Hebrews is the response to foreign people and interest in foreign lands. The four alternatives are summarized in figure 6.

Only one class of societies (weak group, weak grid) can be described as open to outsiders. The attitudes of other societies range from wary to fearful to hostile. According to this model first-century CE Judaism should not be expected to have been actively missionary. This expectation is consistent with recent studies of this subject.

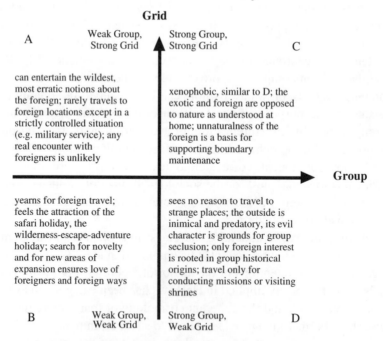

Figure 6. *Paradigmatic responses to foreign people and interest in foreign lands. Adapted from Douglas, 'Cultural Bias', pp. 212-13.*

56. Douglas, 'Cultural Bias', p. 190. Cf. ibid., p. 201; 'the relevant level of analysis is that at which people find it necessary to explain to each other why they behave as they do.'

Goodman distinguished between four levels of religious discourse:

1. informative; imparting a message with 'no clear idea of the action…desired from [the] auditors'
2. 'a mission to educate'; proclaiming a message to promote greater morality or contentment among the auditors without a requirement that the change be accompanied by acceptance of a belief system
3. apologetic; a request for 'recognition by others of the power of a particular divinity without expecting [the] audience to devote themselves to his or her worship'
4. proselytizing; 'as members of a defined group,…to encourage outsiders not only to change their way of life but also to be incorporated within [the] group'.[57]

Only the last of these levels can be characterized accurately as an active, intentional missionary venture. In his examination of the evidence for Jewish missionary activity prior to 100 CE, Goodman argued convincingly that alleged Jewish missions aimed at converting gentiles to Judaism should be viewed as informational, educational, or apologetic efforts, not as proselytism.[58] Those gentiles who sought admission to Judaism were accepted,[59] but Goodman found 'no good reason to suppose that any Jew would have seen value in seeking proselytes in the first century with an enthusiasm like that of the Christian apostles'.[60]

Scot McKnight and Irina Levinskaya reached similar conclusions. While recognizing 'that Jews were not isolationist in their attitudes and relations with Gentiles', McKnight's interpretation of the data was that 'Judaism never developed a clear mission to the Gentiles that had as its goal the conversion of the world'.[61] McKnight found 'no evidence that could lead to the conclusion that Judaism was a "missionary religion" in the sense of aggressive attempts to convert Gentiles or in the sense of self identity'.[62] Levinskaya summarized her examination of the data by stating: 'the sources from the first century do not support the view that

---

57. Goodman, *Mission and Conversion*, pp. 3-4.
58. Goodman, *Mission and Conversion*, pp. 60-90.
59. Goodman, *Mission and Conversion*, p. 86.
60. Goodman, *Mission and Conversion*, p. 90.
61. McKnight, *A Light among the Gentiles*, pp. 116-17.
62. McKnight, *A Light among the Gentiles*, p.117.

there was large scale Jewish missionary activity'.[63]

Louis Feldman's attempt to confirm active Jewish missionary endeavors does not overcome objections raised by McKnight and Goodman. One of Feldman's weaknesses is his dependance on a statement attributed to Jesus: 'Woe to you, scribes and Pharisees, hypocrites, because you travel over the sea and the dry land to make one proselyte, and when he becomes [one], you make him twice as much a son of *gehenna* as yourselves' (Mt. 23.15). Feldman described this saying as 'the most striking passage indicating the zeal with which the Jews pursued their missionary activities'.[64] Reading this saying as objective historical evidence of Jewish missionary enterprise ignores the hyperbolic character of the pronouncement and suggests that Jesus was opposed to gentiles converting to Judaism. The more likely interpretation is that Jesus was criticizing the zeal with which the Pharisees sought to promote their own halakhic interpretations, thereby strengthening their position within Judaism.[65]

Another weakness in Feldman's argument is his dependence on Talmudic materials. 'No one can deny the mention…*especially in rabbinic writings* of the conversion of a considerable number of individuals to Judaism' (emphasis mine).[66] Feldman treated late sources on a par with first-century CE sources (Philo and Josephus), neglecting the fact that the amoraic rabbis, whose words and deeds were preserved in the Talmud, lived in a world vastly different from that of the first century CE. During the amoraic period (220–500 CE) Judaism had become accommodated to the loss of the temple and was confronted by the rise of a prominent, new, monotheistic, missionary religion: Christianity. Consequently, any evidence for Jewish missionary activity dating from the amoraic period can be explained (at least in part) as a reaction to the

---

63. Irina Levinskaya, *The Book of Acts in its First Century Setting*. V. *Diaspora Setting* (Grand Rapids, MI: Eerdmans; Carlisle, U.K.: The Paternoster Press, 1996), p. 49.

64. Feldman, *Jew and Gentile in the Ancient World*, p. 298.

65. Goodman, *Mission and Conversion*, p. 70; Levinskaya, *Diaspora Setting*, pp. 38-39. McKnight interpreted the Matthew text as evidence that Pharisees sought to ensure that those gentiles already approaching Judaism (i.e. God-fearers) would accept circumcision and 'the yoke of the Torah'; *A Light among the Gentiles*, pp. 106-108. Even in this interpretation the activity being described is within the synagogue, not strictly beyond the boundaries of the Jewish community.

66. Feldman, *Jew and Gentile in the Ancient World*, p. 290.

rise of Christianity.[67] Relating the group and grid characteristics of amoraic Judaism to this later Jewish missionary activity would be an interesting exercise, but one beyond the scope of the present study and of questionable relevance to an examination of Hebrews.

Having argued that first-century CE Judaism was not a missionary religion, attention turns to the weak group, weak grid ideal society implicit in the text of Hebrews. Douglas's description of societies in this quadrant suggests that members of the implied society would be involved in a 'search for new areas of expansion',[68] would be more willing to engage actively in meaningful dialogue with outsiders, and, because of their openness to foreigners, would experience less resistance to incorporating converted outsiders into the implied society. These suggestions are consistent with the permeable view of boundaries in Hebrews and with the lack of internal structure within the community of believers. First-century Judaism placed significant obstacles in the path of the prospective convert and, upon conversion, placed the new member permanently at the lower-status end of the social scale. Neither of these conditions is present in the implied society.

A rhetorical study of Hebrews supports the view that the author was an advocate of openness to outsiders. Attridge concluded that 'the exhortation of Hebrews functions to confirm the values and commitments of a community suffering social ostracism, while it *insists that those values require engagement in, not separation from the opposing society*' (emphasis mine).[69] Though Attridge found no conclusive evidence that the author sought to give instruction about the socialization of new members,[70] the advocacy of 'engagement in, not separation from' the outside world is consistent with Douglas's description of the weak group, weak grid attitude toward outsiders.

The various proposals for the background of Hebrews (Table 1) can now be considered in light of the argument that the ideal society being advocated implicitly in the epistle is a weak group, weak grid society, seeks new areas for expansion, is open to interaction with outsiders, and is willing to incorporate fully new members into the community of believers. Strictly sectarian proposals (e.g. that of Buchanan) are least

---

67. Goodman, *Mission and Conversion*, p. 152.
68. Douglas, 'Cultural Bias', p. 213.
69. Attridge, 'Paraenesis in a Homily', p. 223.
70. Attridge, 'Paraenesis in a Homily', p. 218.

compatible with the character of the implied society.[71] Concern that
members would defect, a common proposal, seems inconsistent with a
society that 'loves foreigners and foreign ways'.[72] To a society threat-
ened with massive defection, outsiders should be viewed with suspicion, not curiosity. Attempts to dissuade members from defecting
would be more consistent with a view of the outside as hostile, danger-
ous, or evil.[73] While the arguments presented here do not disprove such
interpretations of Hebrews, fear of apostasy in a weak group, weak grid
society would seem to be an anomaly requiring further explanation.

William Manson's proposal is most in harmony with the analysis
presented in this study. Manson concluded that the author of Hebrews
was 'an ardent adherent to the principles of Stephen and the world-
mission [of Christianity]'.[74] Stephen's view of that world mission was
based on the conviction that 'the call of God had passed from the
Jewish people to embrace humanity at large'.[75] After their companion's
death, 'remnants of Stephen's party began the world-mission of Christianity'.[76] Manson concluded that Stephen's teaching was 'the matrix
within which the theological ideas elaborated in Hebrews first took
shape' and that 'the author of Hebrews will have been a fervent up-
holder of the world-mission gospel'.[77]

Indirect support for Manson's proposal is available in the work of
Goodman. According to Goodman, the true missionary impetus of
Christianity originated among those Christians who first accepted gen-
tiles into their midst indiscriminately.[78] Though he did not name

---

71. DeSilva's sectarian interpretation in 'Hebrews in Social-Scientific Perspective' is likewise set aside.

72. Douglas, 'Cultural Bias', p. 213.

73. A probable example is Gal., where some members of the congregation have
been enticed by 'another gospel' (Gal. 1.6). Jerome Neyrey's study of Galatians
('Bewitched in Galatia: Paul and Cultural Anthropology', *CBQ* 50 [1988], pp. 72-
100 [99], concentrating on the witchcraft accusation against Paul's opponents (Gal.
3.1), concludes that the community reflected in Galatians is a strong group, weak
grid society, the kind of society where outsiders are viewed as predatory and evil.

74. William Manson, *The Epistle to the Hebrews: An Historical and Theological Reconsideration, The Baird Lecture, 1949* (London: Hodder and Stoughton,
1951), p. 160.

75. Manson, *The Epistle to the Hebrews*, p. 31.

76. Manson, *The Epistle to the Hebrews*, p. 37.

77. Manson, *The Epistle to the Hebrews*, p. 44.

78. Goodman, *Mission and Conversion*, p. 170. Goodman described his recon-

Stephen, Goodman's reference to 'the rationalization of the universal mission of the Church' in Acts[79] is consistent with an association between world-mission Christianity and the successors to Stephen. With the numerous similarities between the theology of the author of Hebrews and that of Stephen, including the 'call to "Go out" ',[80] the argument that the author was concerned to promote the world mission of Christianity is plausible.

According to Manson, among the primary doctrinal parallels between Stephen and the author of Hebrews was the view of the Jewish cultus.[81] According to this line of reasoning, the critique of the levitical system in the Epistle to the Hebrews is integral to the purpose of the homily and supports the advocacy of an implied society that was both more open to outsiders and more willing to assimilate fully new members than was first-century C.E. hellenistic Judaism. Viewing this point from the opposite perspective, Douglas stated that 'the most important determinant of ritualism is the experience of closed social groups'.[82] If the author sought to advocate the view of the community of believers as an open social group (supporting an enthusiastic commitment to world mission), coherence would require that he exclude an active ritual cultus from the implied society (or limit that cult severely). The conclusion of this syllogism is true; therefore, the premise is allowed.

Eisenbaum's analysis of Heb. 11 can be cited as further support for a portion of Manson's hypothesis. She concluded that the denationalization of Jewish history in Heb. 11 resulted in a situation where, 'once the Jewish heroes were dislodged from their nationally distinctive roles in history, Gentiles could more easily identify with them as Christian, rather than Jewish, heroes'.[83] In the concluding paragraphs of her study, Eisenbaum stated that 'the author of Hebrews so modified the teleology of biblical history that an opening was created for Gentile Christians to fully identify with scriptural history'.[84] Though employing an independent methodology, and concentrating on a portion of the text of Hebrews outside the cultic section of the epistle, Eisenbaum reached a

---

struction as 'tentative'.

79. Goodman, *Mission and Conversion*, p. 170.
80. Manson, *The Epistle to the Hebrews*, p. 36.
81. Manson, *The Epistle to the Hebrews*, p. 160.
82. Douglas, *Natural Symbols*, p. 14.
83. Eisenbaum, *The Jewish Heroes of Christian History*, p. 3.
84. Eisenbaum, *The Jewish Heroes of Christian History*, p. 225.

conclusion in harmony with the argument presented above: the implied society of Hebrews is open to outsiders and is able to incorporate them fully into the community of believers.

A divergence is evident in Eisenbaum's identification of the recipients of Hebrews. She concluded that the intended original audience consisted of 'several communities', incorporating a mixture of Jews and gentiles;[85] therefore, she would not necessarily endorse the association of Hebrews with Stephen. Despite this reservation, Eisenbaum's conclusion on the function of the denationalization she noted in Heb. 11 is consonant with the conclusions drawn from a group/grid analysis of the idealized implied society.

Although these arguments do not prove that Manson was correct in his assessment of the purpose of Hebrews, they demonstrate that his theory is more consistent with the implicit sociological data in the epistle than are the competing theories. Less explicit theories have been advanced; Moffatt and Attridge went no farther than to state that the author called for greater commitment.[86] By virtue of their lack of specificity, these proposals cannot be excluded based on the results of the present study. Manson's explanation has an advantage over these more nebulous proposals because, by virtue of its greater specificity, Manson's theory is more subject to confirmation or refutation.

Apocalypticism and Conversion in Hebrews

In *Natural Symbols* Douglas sought to explain the source of militant anti-ritualism. She found two sources: apocalypticism and conversion. Apocalypticism is the more revolutionary of the motivations, and apocalyptic movements arise in weak group, strong grid or weak group, weak grid societies.[87] Apocalyptic elements are present in Hebrews. Rigorous definition of the apocalyptic genre is a daunting task,[88] but

85. Eisenbaum, *The Jewish Heroes of Christian History*, pp. 9-10.

86. Moffatt, *Hebrews*, pp. xxiv, xxvi; Attridge, *Hebrews*, p. 13.

87. Douglas, *Natural Symbols*, pp. 146-55. Douglas referred to apocalypticism as millennialism. The latter term is employed in sociological studies in the way that the former is employed in biblical studies; cf. Hillel Schwartz, 'Millenarianism: An Overview', in Mircea Eliade (ed.), *The Encyclopedia of Religion*, IX, pp. 521-22.

88. John J. Collins, *The Apocalyptic Imagination: An Introduction to Jewish Apocalyptic Literature* (The Biblical Resource Series; Grand Rapids, MI: Eerdmans, 2nd edn, 1998), pp. 1-42; Leonard L. Thompson, *The Book of Revelation: Apocalypse and Empire* (New York: Oxford University Press, 1990), pp. 11-34.

John McRay has identified apocalyptic features in Hebrews: the eso-
teric (the treatment of angels and of Melchizedek), the literary nature of
the document, and the symbolic nature of the language (depictions of
Christ as a sacrifice, as the veil in the tabernacle, as the high priest who
passed through the heavens, and as the great shepherd of the sheep).[89]
To this catalogue can be added the perception that the coming of the
Son signaled the 'last days' (1.2) and that the self-sacrifice of the Son
marked 'the consummation of the ages' (9.26).

Despite the presence of these apocalyptic elements, militant apocalypticism fails as an explanation for the critique of the levitical cult in
Hebrews. Douglas's explanation calls for violent, revolutionary rejection of ritual where apocalypticism reigns.[90] Such a vehement, apocalyptic response is evident in the Qumran texts, though this reaction is
anomalous. Douglas described apocalypticism as a weak group
phenomenon, and Rayner explained how apocalypticism could arise in
a strong group, weak grid society.[91] No explanation has been provided
for the case of Qumran: apocalypticism in a strong group, strong grid
society. For this reason, Isenberg and Owen commented that 'this part
of the paradigm needs rethinking'.[92]

Rayner's 'basic predicates' for apocalypticism reveal further limitations on the heuristic value of treating Hebrews as an apocalypse. The
predicates are:

1. The conviction that the present epoch is finite and known to be
   ending shortly.
2. The conviction that the new epoch will be established by the
   external intervention of some powerful agency.
3. The conviction that all men ought to be recognized as moral
   equals.[93]

Although the first two predicates are consistent with the two-ages
scheme detectable in Hebrews, the scheme is modified in the epistle.
The return of Jesus is anticipated as a future event (9.28), but 'the con-

89. McRay, 'Atonement and Apocalyptic in the Book of Hebrews', p. 1.

90. Douglas, *Natural Symbols*, pp. 147, 150.

91. Steve Rayner, 'The Perception of Time and Space in Egalitarian Sects: A
Millenarian Cosmology', in Mary Douglas (ed.), *Essays in the Sociology of Perception* (London: Routledge and Kegan Paul, 1982), pp. 247-74.

92. Isenberg and Owen, 'Bodies, Natural and Contrived', p. 12.

93. Rayner, 'The Perception of Time and Space in Egalitarian Sects', p. 248.

summation of the ages' has occurred already (9.26). How this eschatological configuration would impact the apocalyptic rejection of ritualism is unclear.

Douglas's description of 'conversion' is more useful in an analysis of
Hebrews:

> Anyone who finds himself living in a new social condition must, by the
> logic of all we have seen, find that the cosmology he used in his old
> habitat no longer works. We should try to think of cosmology as a set of
> categories that are in use. It is like lenses which bring into focus and
> make bearable the manifold challenge of experience. It is not a hard
> carapace which the tortoise has to carry forever, but something very
> flexible and easily disjointed. Spare parts can be fitted and adjustments
> made without much trouble. Occasionally a major overhaul is necessary
> to bring the obsolete set of views into focus with new times and new
> company. This is conversion…there is a burden of old, irrelevant rituals
> to be laid aside. They no longer have meaning because the social action
> in which they inhered no longer exists… So the more social change, the
> more radical revision of cosmologies, the more conversion phenomena,
> and the more denigration of ritual.[94]

As has been argued above, in Hebrews the levitical ritual is not deni-
grated but is viewed as terminated. A cultic system that was appropriate
before has been fulfilled in the once-for-all sacrifice of Christ. The
move from non-missionary Judaism to a society committed to world
mission does constitute a significant social change that should be
accompanied by a thorough revision of cosmology. This 'conversion' to
Christianity, as understood by the author, necessitated his thorough
reevaluation of the levitical cultus.

Society and the Levitical Cult in Hebrews

The levitical cultus was not merely a social phenomenon. To treat the
sacrificial system as nothing but a reflection of Jewish society or as a
means to mold individuals into the requisite societal structures would
be a reductionistic neglect of the theological aspects of a form of worship that endured for centuries despite the changing political and social
fortunes of Israel. Conversely, to classify the author's critique of the
cultus solely as a calculated measure to enforce a separation between
his audience and their roots in hellenistic Judaism would be an unwar-

94. Douglas, *Natural Symbols*, pp. 144-45.

ranted overstatement. Douglas rejected the reductionism and the implied determinism involved in such errors: 'it is not intended to imply that a causal relation exists between cosmology as effect and social context as cause. In any social context, it may be assumed that the chains of cause and effect between the structures of social interaction and cosmological and cultural systems which are supporting them are indefinitely interwoven and interdependent.'[95] If the requisite data existed, a study of the understanding of the cultus in the various eras of Israel's history would be a valuable enterprise, but one that is far beyond the present scope.

The purpose of the present study and of this chapter in particular has been to investigate the author's critique of the levitical system as a social phenomenon. In that investigation, the critique has been shown to be a component of a coherent cosmology, and that cosmology is compatible with life in an implied weak group, weak grid society. Further, that view of the implied society supports Manson's proposal for the purpose of Hebrews; members of the implied society are ideally suited for carrying out the world mission of the Church. Other investigations of the critique of the levitical system are possible and would be valuable (e.g. the implications for a comprehensive theory of atonement), but again these avenues lead far beyond the territory traversed here.

Finally, the contrast between the implied society and at least one version of Paul's vision of the church (in Galatians)[96] suggests that Paul and the author of Hebrews might have held different views on the objective and meaning of the mission to the gentiles. Jerome Neyrey's conclusion that Galatians reflects a strong group, weak grid society is not contradictory to a particular approach to missions,[97] but the understanding of the missionary endeavor should differ between the two quadrants (B and D). Douglas's paradigm suggests an hypothesis that Paul viewed the mission in terms of rescuing misplaced persons from peril, while the author of Hebrews conceived of the mission as welcoming and incorporating outsiders into the city of God. This hypothesis is not tested here, rather the new hypothesis suggests an avenue along which to extend the present study in a new direction.[98]

95. Douglas, 'Cultural Bias', p. 247.

96. Neyrey, 'Bewitched in Galatia', pp. 99-100.

97. Douglas, 'Cultural Bias', p. 212.

98. Paul's reference to deliverance 'from the coming wrath' (1 Thess. 1.10) may provide the key to confirming this new hypothesis.

Chapter 6

CONCLUSION

Though he was a poor, simple farmer, Tevye understood the sociological function of ritual. In the monologue with which the musical *Fiddler on the Roof* opens, the central character comments on the intricate network of traditions governing all of life in Anatevka: rules governing sleeping, eating, working, and clothing. By means of these ritualized traditions, roles within the Jewish community were reinforced and the boundary between the villagers and the larger world was marked clearly. The ubiquitous rituals/traditions of *shtetl* life in Anatevka contribute to definition of group and grid. This phenomenon is not restricted to a fictitious village in czarist Russia. Any member of a non-liturgical denomination who has attended worship in a liturgical church (e.g. a Baptist attending a celebration of the divine liturgy in an Orthodox cathedral) knows how the elements of the ritual reinforce grid (the unique role of the priest as celebrant) and group (the visitor as alien). To affiliate with the other community is much more than an intellectual decision or a theological conviction; self-identification as a member of that different community is required, with the new member accepting the community's history, culture, and traditions as his or her own.

Some realignments are necessary (acceptance of the authority of the patriarch is essential for one who wishes to become Orthodox), but others seem less critical (must the liturgy be conducted in Greek, or Arabic, or Church Slavonic instead of English?). Less obvious as ritual, but no less real, are the 'traditions' of the non-liturgical church. Approaching the pastor during the invitation at the close of the worship service is not a purely spontaneous act, but has ritual characteristics (the privileged role of the pastor, the sense of the sacred in terms of time and place, the public nature of the petition for membership). Baptism in the accepted mode may be a vital act of initiation, but does 'walking the aisle' have the same status?

Social realignment, particularly on peripheral issues, complicates the decision to join the new community. Where such peripheral issues are genuinely optional, relaxation of the 'traditional' requirements for membership can ease the transition from outsider to member. Relaxation requires that present members weaken the internal and external boundaries of their community, a process that may require courage and involve risk.

In his implicit advocacy of an ideal society, the author of Hebrews promoted conditions conducive to the entry of outsiders into the community of believers. He conceived of the boundaries of the new community as porous, he placed all (human) members on a single stratum, and he minimized the role of ritual in the spiritual life of the society. The last of these elements of implicit social definition in the ideal society was accomplished in large part through an extended critique of the levitical system, a defining ritual of the society from which the Author and his readers had emerged. Following the author's lead, his readers would be better equipped to carry out the world mission of the church. With the increased exposure to those 'outside the camp' (13.13) incumbent in the world mission, the believers would require courage to face the risk of persecution, but would find security in their faithful lives as citizens of the city of the living God.

BIBLIOGRAPHY

Accordance, computer software, Ver. 2.1, Altamonte Springs, FL: OakTree Software Specialists, 1996.

Attridge, Harold W., 'The Uses of Antithesis in Hebrews 8–10', *HTR* 79 (1986), pp. 1-9.

—*The Epistle to the Hebrews* (Hermeneia; Philadelphia: Fortress Press, 1989).

—'Paraenesis in a Homily (λόγος παρακλήσεως): The Possible Location of, and Socialization in, the "Epistle to the Hebrews" ', *Semeia* 50 (1990), pp. 211-26.

Aulén, Gustaf, *Christus Victor: An Historical Study of the Three Main Types of the Idea of Atonement* (trans. A.G. Hebert; New York: Collier Books, Macmillan Publishing Company, 1986).

Balz, Horst Robert, and Gerhard Schneider (eds.), *Exegetical Dictionary of the New Testament*, I (trans. Virgil P. Howard, James W. Thompson, John W. Medendorp, and Douglas W. Stott; 3 vols; Grand Rapids, MI: Eerdmans, 1990).

Barclay, John M.G., *Jews in the Mediterranean Diaspora: From Alexander to Trajan (323 BCE–117 CE)* (Edinburgh: T. & T. Clark, 1996).

Baumgärtel, Friedrich, and Johannes Behm, 'καρδία', *TDNT*, III, pp. 605-13.

Blond, Georges, 'Clement of Rome', in Raymond Johanny (ed.), *The Eucharist of the Early Christians*, pp. 24-47.

Bock, Darrell L., *Luke 1:1–9:50* (Baker Exegetical Commentary on the New Testament; Grand Rapids: Baker Book House, 1994).

Bruce, F.F., *The Epistle to the Hebrews* (NICNT; Grand Rapids, MI: Eerdmans, 2nd edn, 1990).

Buchanan, George Wesley, *To the Hebrews: A New Translation with Introduction and Commentary* (AB; New York: Doubleday, 1972).

Caquot, André, 'La secte de Qoumrân et le temple (essai de synthèse)', *RHPR* 72 (1992), pp. 3-14.

Carroll, John T., and Joel B. Green, *The Death of Jesus in Early Christianity* (Peabody, MA: Hendrickson, 1995).

Charlesworth, James H., 'A Critical Comparison of the Dualism in 1QS 3:13 4:26 and the "Dualism" Contained in the Gospel of John', in James H. Charlesworth (ed.), *John and the Dead Sea Scrolls* (New York: Crossroad, 1991), pp. 76-106.

Chilton, Bruce, and Jacob Neusner, *Judaism in the New Testament: Practices and Beliefs* (London: Routledge, 1995).

Clapp, Philip S., Barbara Friberg and Timothy Friberg (eds.), *Analytical Concordance of the Greek New Testament*. I. *Lexical Focus* (Baker's Greek New Testament Library; Grand Rapids, MI: Baker Book House, 1991).

Cohen, Shaye J.D. 'Crossing the Boundary and Becoming a Jew', *HTR* 82 (1989), pp. 13-33.

Collins, John J., *The Apocalyptic Imagination: An Introduction to Jewish Apocalyptic*

Literature (The Biblical Resource Series; Grand Rapids, MI: Eerdmans, 2nd edn, 1998).

Cullmann, Oscar, *Early Christian Worship* (trans. A. Stewart Todd and James B. Torrance; SBT; Chicago: Henry Regnery Company, 1953).

Deissmann, Adolf, *Light from the Ancient East: The New Testament Illustrated by Recently Discovered Texts of the Graeco-Roman World* (trans. Lionel R.M. Strachan; New York: George H. Doran Company, 4th edn, 1927).

deSilva, David Arthur, 'Despising Shame: A Cultural-Anthropological Investigation of the Epistle to the Hebrews', *JBL* 113 (1994), pp. 439-61.

—'The Epistle to the Hebrews in Social-Scientific Perspective', *ResQ* 36 (1994), pp. 1-21.

—*Despising Shame: Honor Discourse and Community Maintenance in the Epistle to the Hebrews* (SBLDS, 152; Atlanta: Scholars Press, 1995).

—'Exchanging Favor for Wrath: Apostasy in Hebrews and Patron Client Relationships', *JBL* 115 (1996), pp. 91-116.

Douglas, Mary, *Purity and Danger: An Analysis of Concepts of Pollution and Taboo* (New York: Frederick A. Praeger, Publishers, 1966).

—'Deciphering a Meal', *Daedalus* 101 (1972), pp. 61-81.

—'Cultural Bias', in Mary Douglas, *In the Active Voice* (Routledge and Kegan Paul: London, 1982), pp. 183-254.

—'Introduction to Group/Grid Analysis', in Douglas (ed.), *Essays in the Sociology of Perception*, pp. 1-8.

—*Natural Symbols: Explorations in Cosmology* (New York: Pantheon Books, 3rd edn, 1982).

—'The Background of the Grid Dimension: A Comment', *Sociological Analysis* 50 (1989), pp. 171-76.

Douglas, Mary (ed.), *Essays in the Sociology of Perception* (London: Routledge and Kegan Paul, 1982).

Dunn, James D.G., *Unity and Diversity in the New Testament: An Inquiry into the Character of Earliest Christianity* (London: SCM Press; Valley Forge, PA: Trinity Press International, 2nd edn, 1990).

—*The Partings of the Ways: Between Christianity and Judaism and their Significance for the Character of Christianity* (London: SCM Press; Philadelphia: Trinity Press International, 1991).

Dunnill, John, *Covenant and Sacrifice in the Letter to the Hebrews* (SNTSMS, 75; Cambridge: Cambridge University Press, 1992).

Durkheim, Emile, *The Elementary Forms of the Religious Life* (trans. Joseph Ward Swain; Glencoe, IL: Free Press, 1954).

Ebert, Daniel J., 'The Chiastic Structure of the Prologue to Hebrews', *Trinity Journal* 13 (1992), pp. 163-79.

Ehrman, Bart D., *The New Testament: A Historical Introduction to the Early Christian Writings* (New York: Oxford University Press, 1997).

Eisenbaum, Pamela Michelle, *The Jewish Heroes of Christian History: Hebrews 11 in Literary Context* (SBLDS, 156; Atlanta: Scholars Press, 1997).

Eliade, Mircea (ed.), *The Encyclopedia of Religion* (16 vols.; New York: Macmillan Publishing Company, 1987).

Ellingworth, Paul, *The Epistle to the Hebrews: A Commentary on the Greek Text* (NIGTC; Grand Rapids, MI: Eerdmans; Carlisle, UK: Paternoster Press, 1993).

Ellingworth, Paul, and Eugene Albert Nida, *A Handbook on the Letter to the Hebrews* (UBS Handbook Series; New York: United Bible Societies, 1983).

Elliott, John Hall, *What is Social Scientific Criticism?* (Guides to Biblical Scholarship, New Testament Series, Minneapolis: Fortress Press, 1993).

—'Patronage and Clientage', in Rohrbaugh (ed.), *The Social Sciences and New Testament Interpretation*, pp. 144-56.

Fee, Gordon D., *The First Epistle to the Corinthians* (NICNT; Grand Rapids, MI: Eerdmans, 1987).

Feldman, Louis H., *Jew and Gentile in the Ancient World: Attitudes and Interactions from Alexander to Justinian* (Princeton: Princeton University Press, 1993).

—*Studies in Hellenistic Judaism* (AGJU; Leiden: E.J. Brill, 1996).

Fitzmeyer, Joseph A., *The Gospel According to Luke (I–IX)* (AB; Garden City, NY: Doubleday, 1981).

Freedman, David Noel (ed.), *Anchor Bible Dictionary* (6 vols.; New York: Doubleday, 1992).

Filson, Floyd V., *'Yesterday': A Study of Hebrews in the Light of Chapter 13* (SBT; London: SCM Press, 1967).

Fraade, Steven D., 'Interpretive Authority in the Studying Community at Qumran', *JJS* 44 (1993), pp. 46-69.

García Martínez, F., and Wilfred G.E. Watson (eds. and trans.), *The Dead Sea Scrolls Translated: The Qumran Texts in English* (Leiden: E.J. Brill; Grand Rapids, MI: Eerdmans, 2nd edn, 1996).

Garfiel, Evelyn, *Service of the Heart: A Guide to the Jewish Prayer Book* (Northvale, NJ: Jason Aronson, 1989).

Glaze, R.E., Jr, *No Easy Salvation: A Careful Examination of the Question of Apostasy in Hebrews* (New Orleans: Insight Press, 1966).

Gooch, Paul W., ' "Conscience' in 1 Corinthians 8 and 1" ', *NTS* 33 (1987), pp. 244-54.

Goodman, Martin, *Mission and Conversion: Proselytizing in the Religious History of the Roman Empire* (Oxford: Clarendon Press, 1994).

Gordon, Robert P., 'Better Promises: Two Passages in Hebrews against the Background of the Old Testament Cultus', in Horbury (ed.), *Templum Amicitiae*, pp. 434-49.

Grabbe, Lester L., *Judaism from Cyrus to Hadrian. II. The Roman Period* (Minneapolis: Fortress Press, 1992).

—'Hellenistic Judaism', in Jacob Neusner (ed.) *Judaism in Late Antiquity. II. Historical Syntheses* (Handbook of Oriental Studies: The Near and Middle East; Leiden: E.J. Brill, 1995), pp. 53-83.

Grayston, Kenneth, 'Salvation Proclaimed III. Hebrews 9[11-14]', *ExpTim* 93 (1982), pp. 164-68.

Gross, Jonathan L., and Steve Rayner, *Measuring Culture: A Paradigm for the Analysis of Social Organization* (New York: Columbia University Press, 1985).

Guthrie, George H., *The Structure of Hebrews: A Text-Linguistic Analysis* (NovTSup; Leiden: E.J. Brill, 1994).

Hagner, Donald A., *Hebrews* (NIBC; Peabody, MA: Hendrickson; Carlisle, UK: Paternoster Press, 1995).

Hartley, John E., *Leviticus* (WBC; Dallas, TX: Word Books, 1992).

Hengel, Martin, *Judaism and Hellenism: Studies in their Encounter in Palestine during the Early Hellenistic Period* (trans. John Bowden; 2 vols.; Philadelphia: Fortress Press, 1974).

Horbury, William (ed.), *Templum Amicitiae: Essays on the Second Temple Presented to Ernst Bammel* (Sheffield: Sheffield Academic Press, 1991).

Humbert, J.-B., 'L'espace sacré à Qumrân: Propositions pour l'archéologie', *RB* 101 (1994), pp. 161-214.

Ilan, Tal, *Jewish Women in Greco-Roman Palestine* (Peabody, MA: Hendrickson, 1995).

Isenberg, Sheldon R., and Dennis E. Owen, 'Bodies, Natural and Contrived: The Work of Mary Douglas', *RelSRev* 3 (1977), pp. 1-17.

Jeffers, James S., *Conflict at Rome: Social Order and Hierarchy in Early Christianity* (Minneapolis: Fortress Press, 1991).

Jefford, Clayton N., *Reading the Apostolic Fathers: An Introduction* (Peabody, MA: Hendrickson, 1996).

Jewett, Robert, *Letter to Pilgrims: A Commentary on the Epistle to the Hebrews* (New York: Pilgrim Press, 1981).

Johanny, Raymond (ed.), *The Eucharist of the Early Christians* (trans. Matthew J. O'Connell; New York: Pueblo Publishing Company, 1978).

Johnsson, William George, 'Defilement and Purgation in the Book of Hebrews' (PhD dissertation, Vanderbilt University, 1973).

—'The Cultus of Hebrews in Twentieth-Century Scholarship', *ExpTim* 89 (1978), pp. 104-108.

Kee, Howard Clark, *Knowing the Truth: A Sociological Approach to New Testament Interpretation* (Minneapolis: Fortress Press, 1989).

Kirzner, Yitzchok, and Lisa Aiken, *The Art of Jewish Prayer* (Northvale, NJ: Jason Aronson, 1991).

Kraabel, A.T., 'Unity and Diversity among Diaspora Synagogues', in Levine (ed.), *The Synagogue in Late Antiquity*, pp. 49-60.

Lane, William L., *Hebrews 1–8* (WBC; Dallas: Word Books, 1991).

—*Hebrews 9–13* (WBC; Dallas: Word Books, 1991).

Lehne, Susanne, *The New Covenant in Hebrews* (JSNTSup, 44; Sheffield: JSOT Press, 1990).

Leon, Harry Joshua, *The Jews of Ancient Rome* (Peabody, MA: Hendrickson , updated edn with a new introduction by Carolyn A. Osiek, 1995).

Levine, Baruch A., *Leviticus* (The JPS Torah Commentary; Philadelphia: Jewish Publication Society, 1989).

Levine, Lee I., 'The Second Temple Synagogue: The Formative Years', in Levine (ed.), *The Synagogue in Late Antiquity*, pp. 7-31.

—'Synagogue Officials: The Evidence from Caesarea and its Implications for Palestine and the Diaspora', in Avner Raban and Kenneth G. Holum (eds.), *Caesarea Maritima: A Retrospective after Two Millennia* (Leiden: E.J. Brill, 1996), pp. 392-400.

Levine, Lee I. (ed.), *The Synagogue in Late Antiquity* (Philadelphia: The American Schools of Oriental Research, 1987).

Levinskaya, Irina, *The Book of Acts in its First Century Setting*. V. *Diaspora Setting* (Grand Rapids, MI: Eerdmans; Carlisle, UK: The Paternoster Press, 1996).

Lindars, Barnabas, *The Theology of the Letter to the Hebrews* (NTT; Cambridge: Cambridge University Press, 1991).

Long, Thomas G., *Hebrews* (Int; Louisville: John Knox Press, 1997).

Louw, Johannes P. and Eugene A. Nida (eds.), *Greek English Lexicon of the New Testament Based on Semantic Domains* (2 vols.; New York: United Bible Societies, 2nd edn, 1989).

Lüdemann, Gerd, 'συνείδησις', in Balz and Schneider (eds.), *Exegetical Dictionary of the New Testament*, III, pp. 301-303.

Lust, J., E. Eynikel, K. Hauspie and G. Chamberlain, *A Greek-English Lexicon of the Septuagint* (2 vols.; Stuttgart: Deutsche Bibelgesellschaft, 1992, 1996).

Malina, Bruce J., *The New Testament World: Insights from Cultural Anthropology* (Louisville: Westminster/John Knox Press, 2nd edn, 1993).

—review of *Despising Shame: Honor Discourse and Community Maintenance in the Epistle to the Hebrews* (SBLDS; Atlanta: Scholars Press, 1995), by David Arthur deSilva, in *JBL* 116 (1997), pp. 378-79.

Malina, Bruce J., and Richard L. Rohrbaugh, *Social-Science Commentary on the Synoptic Gospels* (Minneapolis: Fortress Press, 1992).

Manson, William, *The Epistle to the Hebrews: An Historical and Theological Reconsideration, The Baird Lecture, 1949* (London: Hodder and Stoughton, 1951).

Maurer, Christian, 'σύνοιδα, συνείδησις', *TDNT*, VII, pp. 898-919.

McKnight, Scot, *A Light among the Gentiles: Jewish Missionary Activity in the Second Temple Period* (Minneapolis: Fortress Press, 1991).

McRay, John, 'Atonement and Apocalyptic in the Book of Hebrews', *ResQ* 23 (1980), pp. 1-9.

Michaud, Jean-Paul, 'Le passage de l'ancien au nouveau, selon l'épître aux Hébreux', *ScEs* 35 (1983), pp. 33-52.

Milgrom, Jacob, *Leviticus 1–16* (AB; Garden City, NY: Doubleday, 1991).

Moffatt, James, *A Critical and Exegetical Commentary on the Epistle to the Hebrews* (ICC; Edinburgh: T. & T. Clark, 1924).

Moingt, Joseph, 'Prêtre "selon le nouveau testament": à propos d'un livre récent', *RSR* 69 (1981), pp. 573-98.

Moxnes, Halvor, 'Patron-Client Relations and the New Community in Luke Acts', in Neyrey (ed.), *The Social World of Luke Acts: Models for Interpretation*, pp. 241-68.

Neusner, Jacob, *A History of the Mishnaic Law of Women*. V. *The Mishnaic System of Women* (SJLA; Leiden: E.J. Brill, 1980).

—*Judaism: The Evidence of the Mishnah* (Atlanta: Scholars Press, 1988).

—review of *Judaism: Practice and Belief 63 B.C.E.–67 C.E.* (London: SCM Press; Philadelphia: Trinity Press International, 1992), by E. P. Sanders *JSJ* 24 (1993), pp. 317-23.

Neyrey, Jerome H., 'Bewitched in Galatia: Paul and Cultural Anthropology', *CBQ* 50 (1988), pp. 72-100.

—'Ceremonies in Luke–Acts: The Case of Meals and Table Fellowship', in Neyrey (ed.), *The Social World of Luke Acts: Models for Interpretation*, pp. 361-87.

—'Meals, Food, and Table Fellowship', in Rohrbaugh (ed.), *The Social Sciences and New Testament Interpretation*, pp. 159-82.

Neyrey, Jerome H. (ed.), *The Social World of Luke Acts: Models for Interpretation* (Peabody, MA: Hendrickson, 1991).

Nolland, John, *Luke 1–9:20* (WBC; Dallas: Word Books, 1989).

Osiek, Carolyn, and David L. Balch, *Families in the New Testament World: Households and House Churches* (The Family, Religion, and Culture; Louisville: Westminster/John Knox Press, 1997).

Pitt-Rivers, Julian, 'Honour and Social Status', in J.G. Peristiany (ed.), *Honour and Shame: The Values of Mediterranean Society* (Chicago: University of Chicago Press, 1966), pp. 19-77.

Polhill, John B., *Acts* (The New American Commentary; Nashville: Broadman Press, 1992).

Pursiful, Darrell Jeffrey, *The Cultic Motif in the Spirituality of the Book of Hebrews* (Lewiston, NY: Edward Mellen Press, 1993).

Rapske, Brian, *The Book of Acts in its First Century Setting. III. Paul in Roman Custody* (Grand Rapids, MI: Eerdmans; Carlisle, UK: The Paternoster Press, 1994).

Rayner, Steve, 'The Perception of Time and Space in Egalitarian Sects: A Millenarian Cosmology', in Douglas (ed.), *Essays in the Sociology of Perception*, pp. 247-74.

Rohrbaugh, Richard L., ' "Social Location of Thought" as a Heuristic Construct in New Testament Study', *JSNT* 30 (June 1987), pp. 103-19.

Rohrbaugh, Richard L. (ed.), *The Social Sciences and New Testament Interpretation* (Peabody, MA: Hendrickson, 1996).

—'The Pre-Industrial City in Luke–Acts: Urban-Social Relations', in Neyrey (ed.), *The Social World of Luke Acts: Models for Interpretation*, pp. 125-49.

—'The Preindustrial City', in Rohrbaugh (ed*.), The Social Sciences and New Testament Interpretation*, pp. 107-25.

Safrai, S. 'Relations between the Diaspora and the Land of Israel', in Safrai, Stern, Flusser, and van Unnik (eds.), *The Jewish People in the First Century: Historical Geography, Political History, Social, Cultural and Religious Life and Institutions*, pp. 184-215.

—'The Synagogue', in Safrai, Stern, Flusser, and van Unnik (eds.), *The Jewish People in the First Century: Historical Geography, Political History, Social, Cultural and Religious Life and Institutions*, pp. 908-44.

—'The Temple', in Safrai, Stern, Flusser, and van Unnik (eds.), *The Jewish People in the First Century: Historical Geography, Political History, Social, Cultural and Religious Life and Institutions*, pp. 865-907.

Safrai, S., M. Stern, D. Flusser, and W. C. van Unnik (eds.), *The Jewish People in the First Century: Historical Geography, Political History, Social, Cultural and Religious Life and Institutions* (CRINT, Assen, Netherlands: Van Gorcum, 1974).

Sand, Alexander, 'καρδία', in Balz and Schneider (eds.), *Exegetical Dictionary of the New Testament*, II, pp. 249-51.

Sanders, E.P., *Judaism: Practice and Belief 63 BCE–66 CE* (London: SCM Press; Philadelphia: Trinity Press International, 1992).

Schiffman, Lawrence H., 'Communal Meals at Qumran', *RevQ* 10 (1979), pp. 45-56.

—*Reclaiming the Dead Sea Scrolls: The History of Judaism, the Background of Christianity, The Lost Library of Qumran* (Philadelphia: Jewish Publication Society, 1994).

Scholer, John M., *Proleptic Priests: Priesthood in the Epistle to the Hebrews* (JSNTSup, 49; Sheffield: JSOT Press, 1991).

Schürer, Emil, *A History of the Jewish People in the Age of Jesus Christ* (trans. and rev. by Geza Vermes, Fergus Millar, Matthew Black, and Martin Goodman; 4 vols.; Edinburgh: T. & T. Clark, 1973, 1979, 1986, 1987).

Schwartz, Hillel, 'Millenarianism: An Overview', in Eliade (ed.), *The Encyclopedia of Religion*, IX, pp. 521-32.

Scullion, James Patrick, 'A Traditio-Historical Study of the Day of Atonement' (PhD dissertation, Catholic University of America, 1991).

Selby, Gary S., 'The Meaning and Function of Συνείδησις in Hebrews 9 and 10', *ResQ* 28 (1986), pp. 145-54.

Smith, Jonathan Z., 'The Social Description of Early Christianity', *RelSRev* 1 (September 1975), pp. 19-25.

Spicq, Ceslas, *L'épître aux Hébreux*. I. *Introduction* (Paris: Librairie Lecoffre, 1952).

—'L'épître aux Hébreux, Apollos, Jean-Baptiste, les Hellénistes et Qumran', *RevQ* 1 (1959), pp. 365-90.

Stanley, Steve, 'The Structure of Hebrews from Three Perspectives', *TynBul* 45 (1994), pp. 245-71.

Stern, M., 'Aspects of Jewish Society: The Priesthood and other Classes', in Safrai, Stern, Flusser, and van Unnik (eds.), *The Jewish People in the First Century: Historical Geography, Political History, Social, Cultural and Religious Life and Institutions*, pp. 561-630.

Stylianopoulos, Theodore G., 'Shadow and Reality: Reflections on Hebrews 10:1-18', *Greek Orthodox Theological Review* 17 (1972), pp. 215-30.

Swetnam, James, 'On the Imagery and Significance of Hebrews 9,9-10', *CBQ* 28 (1966), pp. 155-73.

—' "The Greater and More Perfect Tent": A Contribution to the Discussion of Hebrews 9,11', *Bib* 47 (1966), pp. 91-106.

—'Christology and the Eucharist in the Epistle to the Hebrews', *Bib* 70 (1989), pp. 74-95.

Thompson, Leonard L., *The Book of Revelation: Apocalypse and Empire* (New York: Oxford University Press, 1990).

Trudinger, L. Paul, 'The Gospel Meaning of the Secular: Reflections on Hebrews 13:10-13', *EvQ* 54 (1982), pp. 235-37.

Vanhoye, Albert, 'Esprit éternel et feu du sacrifice en He 9,14', *Bib* 64 (1983), pp. 263-74.

Wach, Joachim, *Sociology of Religion* (Chicago: University of Chicago Press, 1944).

Walker, Peter W.L., *Jesus and the Holy City: New Testament Perspectives on Jerusalem* (Grand Rapids, MI: Eerdmans, 1996).

Ware, Timothy [Bishop Kallistos Ware], *The Orthodox Church* (Harmondsworth: Penguin Books, 3rd edn, 1993).

—*The Orthodox Way* (Crestwood, NY: St. Vladimir's Seminary Press, 2d edn, 1996).

Welborn, Laurence L., 'Clement, First Epistle of', *ABD*, I, pp. 1055-60.

Wenham, Gordon J., *The Book of Leviticus* (NICOT; Grand Rapids, MI: Eerdmans, 1979).

Williamson, R., 'The Eucharist and the Epistle to the Hebrews', *NTS* 21 (1975), pp. 300-12.

Wong, D.W.F., 'Natural and Divine Order in 1 Clement', *VC* 31 (1977), pp. 81-87.

Wright, N.T. *Christian Origins and the Question of God*. I. *The New Testament and the People of God* (Minneapolis: Fortress Press, 1992).

Young, James A., 'The Significance of Sacrifice in the Epistle to the Hebrews' (ThD dissertation, Southwestern Baptist Theological Seminary, 1963).

Zuesse, Evan M., 'Ritual', in Mircea Eliade (ed.), *The Encyclopedia of Religion*, XII, pp. 405-22.

INDEXES

INDEX OF REFERENCES

OLD TESTAMENT

NEW TESTAMENT

INDEX OF AUTHORS

JOURNAL FOR THE STUDY OF THE NEW TESTAMENT
SUPPLEMENT SERIES